Python
for
NumWorks

Powerful Python programs
and games for the NumWorks
handheld calculator

by John Clark Craig

A Books To Believe In Publication
All Rights Reserved
Copyright 2020 by John Clark Craig

No part of this book may be reproduced or transmitted in any form or by any means, electronic or mechanical, including photocopy, recording or by any information storage and retrieval system, without permission, in writing from the publisher.

Proudly Published in the USA by
Books To Believe In

publisher@bookstobelievein.com

Phone: (303) 794-8888

JohnClarkCraig.com
BooksToBelieveIn.com

First Edition: ISBN: 9798558337716

Foreword
by Romain Goyet
Founder/CEO NumWorks

At their core, computers aren't very smart and only understand a limited set of instructions. For example, the processor of a computer can perform basic operations such as "add 32 and 27", or "which is bigger, this or that number?"

If this is the case, how do we get computers to do amazing things like forecasting weather patterns or generating Hollywood quality visual effects?

Computers must rely on the power of programming languages to accomplish these awe-inspiring tasks. A programming language allows an engineer to utilize more powerful instructions such as "draw a blue rectangle." This more complex instruction is then broken down into a million smaller, less advanced instructions that a computer can actually perform.

Programming languages date back to the '50s, but they have been evolving, just like natural languages. Just like those that humans use, some programming languages have gone extinct, and new ones have emerged from the fusion of pre-existing languages.

A programming language can have different strengths: it can be more or less easy to learn, it can be more or less efficient (in terms of its ability to be smart when generating instructions for the computer), and it can also be more or less widespread.

The Python programming language hits a sweet spot on all of those criterias. It's certainly easy to pick up and quite efficient. It's also used throughout the computer industry, with NASA, CERN, Wikipedia, Google, Facebook and Amazon all making heavy use of the language. It also comes either pre-installed or readily available for most computer environments: Windows, macOS, Linux, etc.

Those three qualities make it an obvious choice for beginners. Its simple syntax makes its learning curve very smooth, even for those new to programming. As an added incentive, there's already a lot of documentation and help readily available. Last but not least, learning Python helps you become more prepared to enter the workforce because professionals already know and use it.

Python has been around for three decades, yet students around the globe are still being taught languages on programmable calculators that will have no use in their future careers. Instead, they learn obscure, proprietary languages that are slow, outdated and kind of pointless. I thought that a change was long overdue. Enter NumWorks, the world's first graphing calculator that can be programmed in Python.

John has seen those languages evolve and he witnessed the rise in popularity of Python. He also believes that Python is an ideal tool for beginners and decided to create a compilation of bite-sized programs for newcomers.

Let me put it simply: there is no better way to learn! Just like learning a spoken language is best done when surrounded by native speakers, learning a computer language is best done when reading small, concrete examples. The variety of topics touched on in this book will keep piquing the curiosity of the reader. In this book, you'll learn how to simulate a loan, how to draw a calendar (it's tricker than it seems!) and how to build a maze!

Even though I have been programming for over two decades, I was captivated when I first cracked open this book!!

Dedication

This book is dedicated to my daughter Jennifer,
one of the many frontline workers struggling
to help others in the battle against Covid 19.

Her health sacrifice and dedication
under intense conditions is an inspiration for all of us.

Acknowledgements

I have great gratitude for several people who helped support efforts to get this book written. Top of the list is Romain Goyet, CEO of NumWorks and creator of this great device.

Romain's expertise and advice were helpful, inspiring and always right on target. I've used and programmed many calculators over the years, but Romain's NumWorks calculator leverages the most popular and easy-to-use programming language in the world in a way that makes calculator programming fun and extremely useful.

Everyone from students to professional engineers will find the power of programming this device to be easy, with a low learning curve, allowing them to focus on what they do best with the calculations instead of being distracted with the complexities of a proprietary programming language.

I can't thank Romain enough for bringing this calculator to the world!

Programs - Table of Contents

1. Calculators and Computers — 12
bin_search.py
factors.py
fibonacci.py
gcd_lcm.py
golden_ratio.py
hex_bin_dec.py
newton.py
primes.py
quadratic.py
rec_pol.py
sim_eq.py
vectors.py

2. Dates and Times — 46
calendar.py
date.py
date_plus.py
julian.py
two_days.py

3. Electronics — 60
ac_voltages.py
bridge.py
freq_wave.py
led_resistor.py
ohms_laws.py
rc_timing.py
z_delta.py
z_parallel.py
z_round.py
z_series.py
z_wye.py

4. Games and Chance — 92
cards.py
coinflips.py
dice.py
digits.py
hunt_dist.py
hunt_news.py
maze.py
memory.py
monty_hall.py
pi_buffon.py
pi_darts.py
pi_graphics.py
random_bytes.py
word_jumble.py
word_perm.py

5. GPS and Navigation   130
area_gps.py
distance_gps.py
great_circle.py
midpoint.py

6. Money and Finances   148
future_val.py
interest.py
loan.py
principal.py
reg_deposits.py

7. Plane Geometry   154
arcs.py
area_3p.py
area_3s.py
area_np.py
circle.py
divide_line.py
lines.py
rotate.py
triangles.py
triangles_3p.py
two_points.py

8. Space Geometry   184
coord_3d.py
rotate_3d.py
triangles_3d.py
volume_4p.py

9. Space Sciences   200
antenna_aim.py
moon.py
moon_img.py
pennies.py
radioisotope.py
relativity.py
station_gravity.py
sun_elev.py
sun_loc.py

10. Other Useful Programs   224
concrete.py
laser_distance.py
secret.py
wind_chill.py

Introduction

The NumWorks calculator is, in several ways, an improvement over the Texas Instruments and Casio calculators. Those other calculators have been with us for several decades now, with only a very, very slow evolution in their capabilities. On the other hand, consider a few of the NumWorks progressive new features and its innovative design.

The NumWorks calculator's keyboard and user interface is modeled after standard game controllers, making its learning curve so much quicker for today's students. The whole calculator is open sourced - even the plastic body can be 3D printed using publicly available STL files. But its support of Python takes its power and usefulness to a whole new level.

Python is arguably now the world's most popular programming language, for everyone from beginners to top professionals. Like the NumWorks calculator, its learning curve is short due to its leaner, cleaner, simpler syntax. Python, and the NumWorks calculator, are both powerful enough to support the efforts of engineers working at NASA on the most demanding calculation tasks, and yet they easily support the ease of learning and first use that greatly aid today's students.

MicroPython is a substantial subset of the full Python language, and it's a perfect match for the calculations required by programmable calculators. Learn MicroPython and a person has a huge head start on computer programming at all levels. Other old school calculators use unique, proprietary programming languages that don't serve future educational and workplace requirements.

This book is a collection of real-world Python programs written explicitly for the NumWorks calculator. Because of the nature of Python, these programs are short, easy to read, easy to enter into your calculator, and most importantly easy to understand. They provide a great way to enhance the computational power of the NumWorks calculator, and to help beginners learn a standardized, powerful, and very popular programming language.

The programs are organized into subject areas to meet varying interests and goals. A set of money calculations helps students grasp personal finance concepts. Another set of programs covers electronics fundamentals. Two and three dimensional analytical geometry programs support today's game creation challenges, and so on. Most everyone will find programs of interest in more than one subject area.

1.

Calculators and Computers

The programs in this chapter cover a lot of the standard calculations that calculators and computers can do, and that you might find useful for your studies or on the job. The programs vary from a fast way to find prime numbers, to solving simultaneous equations, finding roots of equations, providing a complete set of vector functions, and more.

bin_search.py

This program finds roots of a function, or where the function crosses the x-axis at y=0. Edit your function of x in the appropriately named function f(x), at the top of the listing. Here's the function we'll work with in the example:

$$y = x^3 - 5x^2 + 2x + 4$$

One way to calculate a power of x in Python is with two asterisks, and that's what we'll use in the example. (The other way is to use the pow() function in the math library.)

A quick plot of this function on your NumWorks calculator shows the function has three roots that lie somewhere between -1 and +5 on the X axis. This program will help you find those roots fast and efficiently.

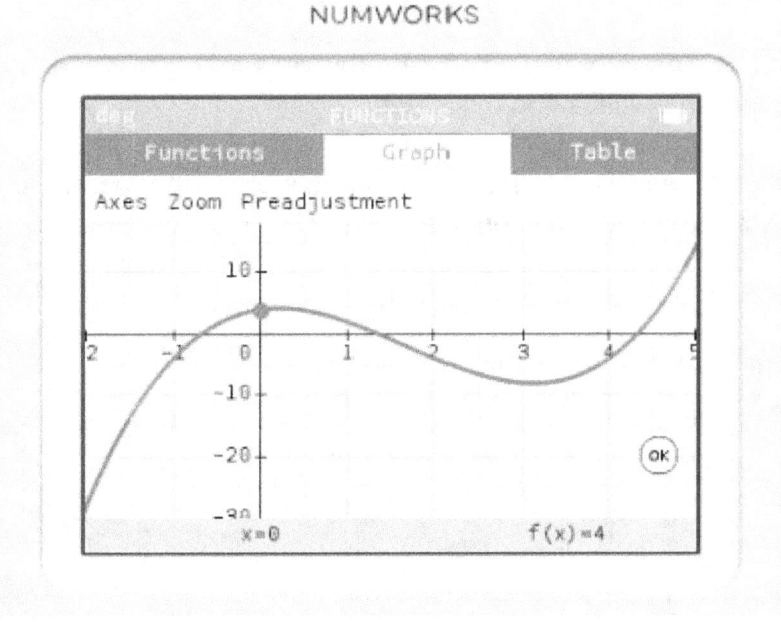

The zero() function in this program is passed two values for x. If there's one or more roots between these values, one of them will be returned. In this example, since we know the three roots are between -1 and 0, 1 and 2, and 4 and 5, the zero() function is called three times to find all three roots. A fourth call to zero() demonstrates that "nan" (not a number) is returned if no root is found in the specified interval.

The binary search cuts the interval between x1 and x2 in half, calculates y at that midpoint, then determines if a root must lie somewhere to the left or to the right of that midpoint. The value of x1 is replaced with the midpoint value in one case, and x2 is replaced otherwise. The search is repeated within this tighter interval, over and over, until the difference between x1 and x2 approaches zero, at the root value of x.

```
>>> from bin_search import *
-0.6813306436049775
1.3579263675185
4.323404276086478
nan
>>>
```

Edit the function at the top of the listing, and the calls to f(x) at the end of the listing to find roots in various intervals along the x axis.

Or, as a challenge to test your Python skills, try changing the program to prompt for two values for x, calculate a root between them, and loop back to repeat the process.

```python
# bin_search.py
def f(x):
    return x**3-5*x**2+2*x+4

def zero(x1,x2):
    lst=0
    y1=f(x1)
    y2=f(x2)
    while 1:
        if y1*y2>0:
            return float("nan")
        x=(x1+x2)/2
        y=f(x)
        if y1*y>0:
            x1=x
            y1=f(x1)
        else:
            x2=x
            y2=f(x2)
        if x1-x2!=lst:
            lst=x1-x2
        else:
            return x

print(zero(-2,0))
print(zero(1,2))
print(zero(6,2))
print(zero(8,9))
```

factors.py

This program finds all the factors of an integer. The factors() function is passed an integer, and it returns a list of all its prime factors.

For example, the prime factors of 32 are five 2's, the prime factors of 12345 are 3, 5, and 823, and the prime factors of 123454321 are 41, 41, 271, and 271:

```
>>> from factors import *
Enter n: 32
[2, 2, 2, 2, 2]
Enter n: 12345
[3, 5, 823]
Enter n: 123454321
[41, 41, 271, 271]
Enter n: 
```

When I first created this program, the factors were found by dividing by all numbers from 2 to the given number to find those that would divide evenly.

This worked great for relatively small integers, but it slowed way down for numbers in the tens of thousands or greater. To speed things up (a lot!) I borrowed the next_prime() function from elsewhere in this book, and checked only for divisibility by prime numbers, and only up to the square root of the given integer. This added a little length to the code listing, but the much speedier results were worth it.

```python
# factors.py
def factors(n):
  fac=[]
  m=2
  pr=2
  while n>1:
    if n%m==0:
      fac.append(m)
      n//=m
    else:
      pr=next_prime(pr)
      m=pr
      if m*m>n:
        fac.append(n)
        break
  return fac

def isPrime(n):
  if n%2==0:
    return False
  m=3
  while m<=n/m:
    if n%m==0:
      return False
    m+=2
  return True

def next_prime(n):
  p=n+1
  while isPrime(p)==False:
    p+=1
  return p

while True:
  s=input("Enter n: ")
  if s=="":
    break
  n=int(s)
  print(factors(n))
```

fibonacci.py

The fibonacci sequence is fascinating, and this program lets you explore its features interactively. Starting with any two integers, where zero and one are often what is chosen, if you add them together to add to the list, then add the last two numbers on that list to get the next, and so on, you end up with a ratio between the last two numbers on the list that approaches the golden ratio.

Search the Internet to learn more about the golden ratio, as there are a lot of curious facts where the explanation at first doesn't seem reasonable. For example, the golden ratio is exactly the same as 2 * sin(54 degrees). The reason has to do with a pentagon shape, but I'll let you discover those details for yourself.

Another interesting fact is that you don't need to start with 0 and 1 to form a Fibonacci sequence. In fact, you can start with any two numbers, positive or negative, integer or float, and the ratio of the last two numbers on the list will quickly approach the golden ratio. That's weird. And you've just got to try it!

Here's the result of starting with 0 and 1, and iterating to grow the sequence 20 times.

```
>>> from fibonacci import *
Enter a: 0
Enter b: 1
Number of additions: 20
a:    6765.000000000001
b:    10946.0
a / b:    0.618033985017358
b / a:    1.618033998521803
Golden:   1.618033988749895
>>> 
```

As you can see, the ratio of 10946 to 6765 is very close to the golden ratio. (The golden ratio can also be calculated as one plus the square root of five all divided by two, and that's how the more exact value is calculated in the last line of the output.)

Next, start with -17.3 and 98.75, and after just 20 additions the ratio can also be seen to be quickly approaching the golden ratio:

```
>>> from fibonacci import *
Enter a: -17.3
Enter b: 98.75
Number of additions: 20
a:   595712.45
b:   963883.0
a / b:    0.6180339833776506
b / a:    1.618034002814613
Golden:   1.618033988749895
>>>
```

```python
# fibonacci.py
a=float(input("Enter a: "))
b=float(input("Enter b: "))
n=int(input("Number of additions: "))
for i in range(n):
    a,b=b,a+b
print("a: ",a)
print("b: ",b)
print("a / b:  ",a/b)
print("b / a:  ",b/a)
print("Golden: ",(1+5**.5)/2)
```

gcd_lcm.py

This program finds the GCD (greatest common divisor) and the LCM (least common multiple) of two integers. The GCD of two integers is the largest positive integer that divides evenly into both. The LCM of two integers is the smallest positive integer that is a multiple of both. It turns out that the product of the two numbers is the product of the LCM and the GCD.

For example, given the integers 24 and 56, we find their GCD is 8, and their LCM is 168.

```
>>> from gcd_lcm import *
Enter a: 24
Enter b: 56
GCD:    8
LCM:    168
>>>
```

```python
# gcd_lcm.py
def gcd(a,b):
    while 1:
        c=a-b*int(a/b)
        a,b=b,c
        if not c:
            return a

def lcm(a,b):
    return int(abs(a*b/gcd(a,b)))

a=int(input("Enter a: "))
b=int(input("Enter b: "))
print("GCD: ",gcd(a,b))
print("LCM: ",lcm(a,b))
```

golden_ratio.py

Search on the Internet for fascinating information about the Golden Ratio (GR), and you'll discover there are multiple ways to calculate this number. Perhaps the most direct calculation is to use this formula:

$$GR = \frac{1 + \sqrt{5}}{2}$$

Another way to calculate GR is with the Fibonacci Sequence (see the fibonacci.py program.)

In this program a simple iteration that starts with any number is used to fairly quickly converge on the value of the Golden Ratio. The GR is equal to 1 + 1/GR, which provides a slick way to iterate to its value.

For example, starting with the number -123.4567 the GR is found after just 40 iterations:

```
>>> from golden_ratio import *
Enter any number: -123.4567
Iterations:  40
Golden:    1.618033988749895
Exact:     1.618033988749895
>>>
```

```python
# golden_ratio.py
x=float(input("Enter any number: "))
y,n=0,0
while x!=y:
    x,y,n=1+1/x,x,n+1
print("Iterations: ",n)
print("Golden:     ",x)
print("Exact:      ",(1+5**.5)/2)
```

hex_bin_dec.py

Computers use bits and bytes and numbers in hexadecimal and binary format all the time. This program shows how a number can easily be converted to and from any of these formats.

For example, the decimal number 234 is the same as hexadecimal 0xEA, and it's the same as the binary number 0b11101010. The program asks for input in any of the formats. Just press enter to skip the unknown formats. All three formats are displayed as output:

```
>>> from hex_bin_dec import *


Input one known value

Hexadecimal:
Binary:
Decimal: 234
Hex:   0xEA
Bin:   0b11101010
Dec:   234
>>> 
```

Note that there's a simpler way to convert hexadecimal or binary numbers to decimal. At the >>> prompt simply enter the value, making sure you add the appropriate prefix of either "0x" or "0b", and the decimal value will be displayed. Hexadecimal values can be entered in either upper or lower case. Here are a few examples:

```
Dec:   234
>>> 0xeb
235
>>> 0xEB
235
>>> 0b10101
21
>>> 0xABCDEFABCDEF
188900977659375
>>> 0b11100010101110001110001
7429233
>>>
```

The last few lines of the program show how to format a decimal integer for output in all three number formats.

```python
# hex_bin_dec.py
print("\n\nInput one known value\n")
h=input("Hexadecimal: ")
n=int(h,16) if h else 0
if not n:
  b=input("Binary: ")
  n=int(b,2) if b else 0
  if not n:
    d=input("Decimal: ")
    n=int(d) if d else 0
print("Hex: ","0x{:X}".format(n))
print("Bin: ","0b{0:b}".format(n))
print("Dec: ",n)
```

newton.py

The bin_search.py program found the roots of a function f(x) using a binary, "split in half" search algorithm. This program also finds roots of a function of x, but it uses Newton's method, a really cool algorithm that in many cases finds roots extremely efficiently.

Newton's method is an iterative method that uses the slope of the function (also known as the first derivative) to help aim at where the function crosses the x axis. Here's the formal definition, where f'(x) is the slope, or derivative, of f(x).

$$x_{next} = x - \frac{f(x)}{f'(x)}$$

To demonstrate this program, we'll find the three roots of the same function of x as in the bin_search.py program:

$$y = x^3 - 5x^2 + 2x + 4$$

A quick sketch of this function in your NumWorks calculator shows there are three roots between -2 and +5 along the x axis.

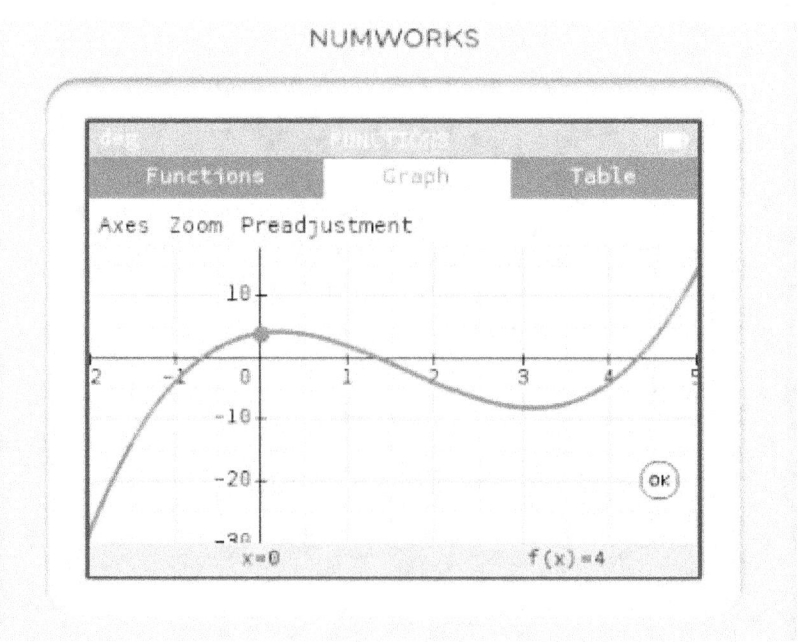

The program calls the zero() function three times, passing in a rough guess as to where each root is. The program zeros in on each of the roots in just a few iterations.

Notice the commented out function named slope(x). There are two functions to calculate the slope, or first derivative, of f(x), and you should comment out one or the other. The first version of slope() is more flexible, in that it doesn't need redefining every time the f(x) function is redefined. The second version is edited specifically for every f(x) if you happen to know the exact first derivative. A little Calculus goes a long way here, but just use the other function, as shown, if finding first derivatives feels like a slippery slope to you at this point. So to speak.

```
>>> from newton import *
-0.6813306436049774
1.3579263675185
4.323404276086477
>>>
```

```
# newton.py
def f(x):
    return x**3-5*x**2+2*x+4

def slope(x):
    dx=0.00001
    dy=f(x+dx)-f(x)
    return dy/dx

##def slope(x):
##    return 3*x*x-10*x+2
```

```
def zero(x):
  xlast=x+1
  while xlast!=x:
    xlast=x
    x=x-f(x)/slope(x)
  return x

print(zero(-1))
print(zero(1))
print(zero(4))
```

primes.py

This program finds n prime numbers with the search starting at any given integer. Prime numbers are those integers that can be divided evenly only by 1 and itself. For example, 7 is prime, 8 is not as it can be divided evenly by 2, and 9 is not because it can be divided by 3.

The program provides two useful functions that work together, or you can call them separately if desired. The first function, isPrime() simply returns True if an integer passed to it is prime, and False otherwise. The function next_prime() is passed any integer which it increments until the next prime number is found.

Here's an example run where five prime numbers starting at 10,000 are found:

```
>>> from primes import *
Enter starting n: 10000
Find how many primes: 5
10007
10009
10037
10039
10061
Enter starting n:
```

```python
# primes.py
def isPrime(n):
    if n%2==0:
        return False
    m=3
    while m<=n/m:
        if n%m==0:
            return False
        m+=2
    return True
```

```
def next_prime(n):
  p=n+2 if n%2 else n+1
  while isPrime(p)==False:
    p+=2
  return p

while 1:
  try:
    x=int(input('Enter starting n: '))
  except:
    break
  try:
    count=int(input('How many primes: '))
  except:
    break

  while count>0:
    count-=1
    x=next_prime(x)
    print(x)
```

quadratic.py

The quadratic formula lets us find the roots of a quadratic function. This program calculates those roots, if they exist.

Consider the following parabolic (quadratic) function, as sketched on your NumWorks calculator:

$$f(x) = 3x^2 - 9x + 4$$

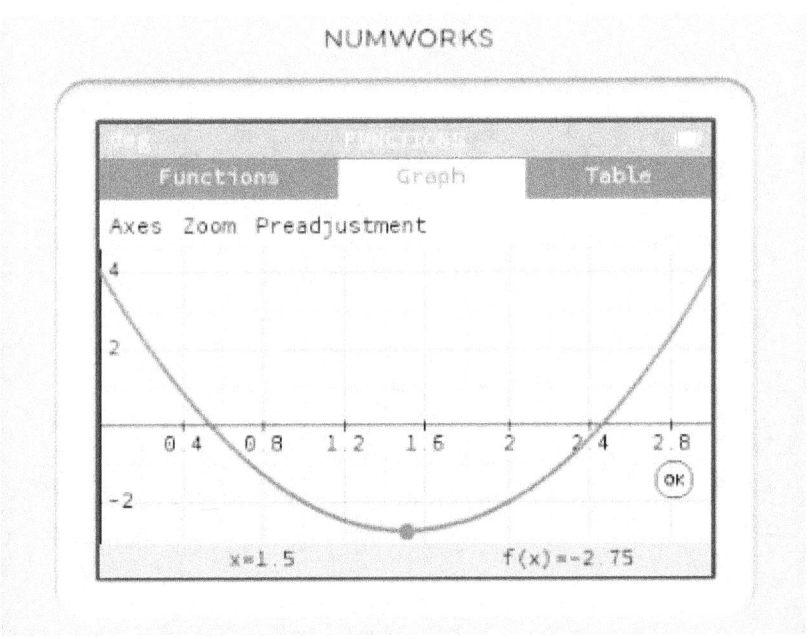

You pass the three values of a, b, and c that form this equation to the roots function, and if the two roots exist a message is returned listing them both.

```
>>> from quadratic import *
Roots:
0.5425728922436619
2.457427107756338
>>>
```

Based on the discriminant, the variable d in the roots() function, there may be zero or just one root in some cases. A message indicating this result is returned if so.

```
# quadratic.py
from math import *

def roots(a,b,c):
  d=b*b-4*a*c
  if d<0:
    return "No real roots"
  elif d== 0:
    return "One root: {}".format(-b/(2*a))
  else:
    x1=(-b-sqrt(d))/(2*a)
    x2=(-b+sqrt(d))/(2*a)
    return "Roots:\n{}\n{}".format(x1,x2)

print(roots(3,-9,4))
```

rec_pol.py

Complex numbers are part of NumWorks Python, making it easy to solve many advanced electronics and other engineering calculations. However, it is often convenient to be able to convert quickly and easily between cartesian, or rectangular, coordinates and standard polar coordinates, where the angle is expressed in degrees.

When the program starts you'll see a message prompting you to press either "1" or "2" to select the desired conversion based on the known data. Note that this program uses the keydown() function to act on a key press in real time. That is, the program doesn't wait for the EXE or OK key to be pressed. Instead, the program proceeds instantly as soon as you press either the "1" key or the "2" key. This can be very handy in some games and other types of programs you create on your NumWorks calculator.

One word of caution however. At the time this book is being written, the NumWorks online simulator does not process the keydown() function correctly. Use it only on your calculator.

For example, to convert a polar point of 17 at an angle of 40 degrees, first press "2" and then enter the data.

```
>>> from rec_pol import *

Press key for known..
(1)   x,y
(2)   r,θ

r: 17
deg: 40
```

The rectangular version of this polar number pair is calculated and both versions of the value are displayed.

```
x:    13.02275553302263
y:    10.92738936467117

r:    17.0
θ:    40.0

>>>
```

This program makes these conversions easy, and it also provides a working demonstration of the keydown() function that allows for real-time monitoring of your key presses while a program is running. The key() function uses the keydown() function to wait for a press of either the [1] or the [2] key on your NumWorks keyboard. A press of [1] indicates you have a rectangular notation value to be converted to polar, and a press of [2] means the opposite conversion is desired.

Here are the equations used to make the conversions. Note that the polar angle is calculated in radians in Python, but the degrees() math function allows us to easily convert it.

$$x = r \cos \theta \qquad r = \sqrt{x^2 + y^2}$$
$$y = r \sin \theta \qquad \theta = \operatorname{atan}\left(\frac{y}{x}\right)$$

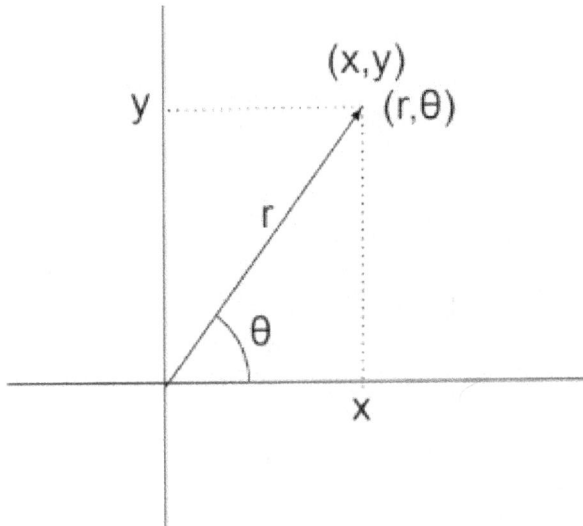

The imported ion module is required when you want to use the keydown() function to watch for key presses when a program is running. This program watches only for the keys labeled "1" and "2" to be pressed, but the NumWorks manual lists codes for all the keys.

Note the special Unicode string for creating the Greek character theta. If you need other special characters in your program creations, check online for tables of Unicode characters. There are a lot of them, and several types of encoding, so be sure to experiment until you get NumWorks Python to display your special characters correctly.

```
# rec_pol.py
from ion import *
from math import *

def key():
    while True:
        if keydown(KEY_ONE):
            return 1
        if keydown(KEY_TWO):
            return 2
```

```
theta="\u03B8"
print("\nPress key for known..")
print("(1)  x,y")
print("(2)  r,"+theta+"\n")
n=key()
if n==1:
  x=float(input("x: "))
  y=float(input("y: "))
if n==2:
  r=float(input("r: "))
  t=radians(float(input("deg: ")))
  x=r*cos(t)
  y=r*sin(t)
r=(x*x+y*y)**.5
t=degrees(atan2(y,x))
print("\n"*3)
print("x: ",x)
print("y: ",y)
print("\nr: ",r)
print(theta+": ",t)
print("\n"*3)
```

sim_eq.py

This program solves simultaneous equations of any size, although too many equations/unknowns can be hard to work with, and it could slow your calculator to a crawl. Most of the time people work with size 2, 3, or 4 simultaneous equations, and this program handles those well.

For example, given the following two equations, what are the values of x and y that satisfy them both?

$$3x + 4y = 5$$
$$6x + 5y = 4$$

The program first prompts for the number of equations, then asks for the coefficients and the constant for each of them in turn, as shown here for our example:

```
>>> from sim_eq import *
Number of equations: 2

Eq 1 Coef 1: 3
Eq 1 Coef 2: 4
Constant:    5

Eq 2 Coef 1: 6
Eq 2 Coef 2: 5
Constant:    4
```

When you enter the last constant, the answers are found and displayed as A1, A2, ... and so on.

```
deg                    PYTHON
Eq 1 Coef 1: 3
Eq 1 Coef 2: 4
Constant:    5

Eq 2 Coef 1: 6
Eq 2 Coef 2: 5
Constant:    4

A1 = -1.0
A2 = 2.0
>>>
```

If you check and plug in -1 and 2 for x and y in the original equations, you'll see that both equations are satisfied.

```
# sim_eq.py
n=int(input("Number of equations: "))
a=[]
for j in range(n):
  coef=[]
  print("")
  for i in range(n):
    p="Eq {} Coef {}: ".format(j+1,i+1)
    x=float(input(p))
    coef.append(x)
  k=float(input("Constant:    "))
  coef.append(k)
  a.append(coef)
```

```python
for j in range(n):
  ok=False
  for i in range(n):
    if i>=j:
      if a[i][j]:
        ok=True
        break
  if not ok:
    print("\nNo solution")
  else:
    for k in range(n+1):
      a[j][k],a[i][k]=a[i][k],a[j][k]
    y=1/a[j][j]
    for k in range(n+1):
      a[j][k]*=y
    for i in range(n):
      if i!=j:
        y=-a[i][j]
        for k in range(n+1):
          a[i][k]+=y*a[j][k]
if ok:
  print("")
  for i in range(n):
    print("A{} = {}".format(i+1,a[i][n]))
```

vectors.py

If you work with vectors this program can come in very handy. Nine different functions cover all the basics of processing one, two, or three 3D vectors at a time.

The functions are generally very short and efficient, and over half of the source listing handles inputting vector values, calling the functions, and outputting results. If you are working with only one or two of these functions, perhaps calling them from a program of your own creation, feel free to just type in the functions themselves to save time and memory.

Note that the cross() and stp() functions work only in three dimensions. All the other functions can also work in two dimensions. Just pass in shorter lists as vectors.

For a working example we'll set the first vector to [3,-2,5], the second to [4,4,0], and the third to [6,3,7]. Each function is called, passing from one to three of these vectors, and the results are output. There's too much to put on one screen, so I added "Press OK" for continuing the action after each set of function calls. You can take out those input lines and just scroll to see all the answers if you wish.

First step is to start the program running and enter the three vectors:

```
Vectors:

V1 x: 3
V1 y: -2
V1 z: 5
V2 x: 4
V2 y: 4
V2 z: 0
V3 x: 6
V3 y: 3
V3 z: 7
```

The results of the add(), sub(), and dot() functions are displayed first, and you are prompted to continue:

```
Add
[7.0, 2.0, 5.0]

Sub
[-1.0, -6.0, 5.0]

Dot product
4.0

Press OK
```

The next three functions are called and displayed, along with one more prompt to continue:

```
Angle between
83.41322444637056

Cross product
[-20.0, 20.0, 20.0]

Scalar triple product
80.0

Press OK
```

Finally, the last three function results are displayed, and the normal shell prompt appears:

```
mul(v1,3)
[9.0, -6.0, 15.0]

mag(v1)
6.164414002968976

unit(v1)
[0.4866642633922877, -0.32444:
>>>
```

The vectors are stored in lists, each containing three numbers. The mul() function requires an integer or float number to multiply vector V1 by, so I just used a 3 to demonstrate the action.

```
# vectors.py
from math import *

def add(v1,v2):
   return [a+b for a,b in zip(v1,v2)]

def sub(v1,v2):
   return [a-b for a,b in zip(v1,v2)]

def dot(v1,v2):
   return sum([a*b for a,b in zip(v1,v2)])

def ang(v1,v2):
   m1=sum(i*i for i in v1)**.5
   m2=sum(i*i for i in v2)**.5
   d=sum([a*b for a,b in zip(v1,v2)])
   return degrees(acos(d/m1/m2))
```

```python
def cross(v1,v2):
    a,b,c=v1
    d,e,f=v2
    return [b*f-c*e,c*d-a*f,a*e-b*d]

def stp(v1,v2,v3):
    a,b,c=v1
    d,e,f=v2
    g,h,i=v3
    p=a*e*i+b*f*g+c*d*h
    m=a*f*h+b*d*i+c*e*g
    return p-m

def mul(v,n):
    return [i*n for i in v]

def mag(v):
    return sum(i*i for i in v)**.5

def unit(v):
    m=sum(i*i for i in v)**.5
    return [i/m for i in v]

print("\nVectors:\n")

# Enter first vector
x=float(input("V1 x: "))
y=float(input("V1 y: "))
z=float(input("V1 z: "))
v1=[x,y,z]

# Enter second vector
x=float(input("V2 x: "))
y=float(input("V2 y: "))
z=float(input("V2 z: "))
v2=[x,y,z]
```

```python
# Enter third vector
x=float(input("V3 x: "))
y=float(input("V3 y: "))
z=float(input("V3 z: "))
v3=[x,y,z]

v=add(v1,v2)
print("\n\nAdd\n{}\n".format(v))
v=sub(v1,v2)
print("Sub\n{}\n".format(v))
d=dot(v1,v2)
print("Dot product\n{}\n".format(d))
input("Press OK")
a=ang(v1,v2)
print("\n\nAngle between\n{}\n".format(a))
c=cross(v1,v2)
print("Cross product\n{}\n".format(c))
s=stp(v1,v2,v3)
print("Scalar triple prod\n{}\n".format(s))
input("Press OK")
d=mul(v1,3)
print("\n\nmul(v1,3)\n{}\n".format(d))
m=mag(v1)
print("mag(v1)\n{}\n".format(m))
u=unit(v1)
print("unit(v1)\n{}\n".format(u))
```

2.

Dates and Times

How old are you today? No, I mean how exactly how many days old are you today? And what day of the week were you born?

These are the types of questions the programs in this chapter will let you answer with ease.

calendar.py

The NumWorks calculator doesn't have (at the time of this writing) a built-in clock or calendar system, but it's easy to create some of these parts, such as this one-month, single-page calendar.

At the heart of this program is a function that returns the Julian Day Number for any date in the range of years from 1582 to 4000. This function, named jd(), is explained in more detail later in this chapter, but here it is used to determine the number of days in any given month, and the day of the week for any date. From this information we can format all the days in a given month into an easy-to-read one-month calendar.

Men first landed on the Moon on July 20, 1969. We can run this program to see the full layout of July, 1969 and easily determine that the 20th was a Sunday.

```
# calendar
def jd(m,d,y):
  if m<3:
    y-=1
    m+=12
  a=int(y/100)
  b=2-a+int(a/4)
  e=int(365.25*(y+4716))
  f=int(30.6001*(m+1))
  return b+d+e+f-1524.5

m=int(input("Month (1-12): "))
y=int(input("Year (1582-4000): "))
d1=int(jd(m,1,y))
dw=(d1+2)%7
m2=m+1 if m<12 else 1
y2=y if m<12 else y+1
d2=int(jd(m2,1,y2))
dm=d2-d1
mo=["Jan","Feb","Mar","Apr","May","Jun",
  "Jul","Aug","Sep","Oct","Nov","Dec"]
n=0
sp=" "
s='\n'*5
s+=sp*2+mo[m-1]+sp+str(y)+"\n\n"
s+="  Su  Mo  Tu  We  Th  Fr  Sa"
s+="\n"+sp*4*dw
while n<dm:
  n+=1
  dw+=1
  t=sp*3 if n<10 else sp*2
  s+=t+str(n)
  if dw%7==0:
    s+="\n"
s+="\n"
print(s)
```

date.py

This program uses the Julian Day Number function to calculate the day of the week and the day of the year for a date in the year range from 1582 to 4000. The jd() function is described in more detail elsewhere in this chapter.

For example, July 20, 1969 (the day man first ventured onto the Moon's surface) was a Sunday, and it was the 201st day of the year, as shown in the following output.

```
>>> from date import *
Month (1-12): 7
Day (1-31): 20
Year (1582-4000): 1969

7/20/1969
Day of week:   Sun
Day of year:   201
>>>
```

The day of the year is found by subtracting the Julian Day Number for December 31 of the previous year from the selected day's Julian Day Number.

```
# date
def jd(m,d,y):
    if m<3:
        y-=1
        m+=12
    a=int(y/100)
    b=2-a+int(a/4)
    e=int(365.25*(y+4716))
    f=int(30.6001*(m+1))
    return b+d+e+f-1524.5
```

```
m=int(input("Month (1-12): "))
d=int(input("Day (1-31): "))
y=int(input("Year (1582-4000): "))
dj=int(jd(m,d,y))
dn=((dj+2)%7)*3
dw="SunMonTueWedThuFriSat"
print("\n{}/{}/{}".format(m,d,y))
print("Day of week: ",dw[dn:dn+3])
dy=dj-int(jd(12,31,y-1))
print("Day of year: ",dy)
```

date_plus.py

This program calculates a date that is a given number of days added to a starting date. For example, the Moon landing occurred on July 20, 1969. What was the date 10,000 days in the future from that day? As shown in the output, December 5, 1996 is the date "way out in the future" from the day we landed on the Moon.

```
>>> from date_plus import *
Month (1-12): 7
Day (1-31): 20
Year (1582-4000): 1969
Number of days: 10000
12/5/1996
>>>
```

To perform this calculation the starting date is converted to its Julian Day Number using the jd() function, the number of days is added to create a second Julian Day Number, and the mdy() function converts that number back to a date. These two functions are described in more detail in the julian.py program in this chapter.

```python
# date_plus.py
from math import *

def jd(m,d,y):
  if m<3:
    y-=1
    m+=12
  a=int(y/100)
  b=2-a+int(a/4)
  e=int(365.25*(y+4716))
  f=int(30.6001*(m+1))
  return b+d+e+f-1524.5

def mdy(jd):
  z=int(jd+.5)
  f=jd+.5-z
  if z<2299161:
    a=z
  else:
    t=int((z-1867216.25)/36524.25)
    a=z+1+t-int(t/4)
  b=a+1524
  c=int((b-122.1)/365.25)
  g=int(365.25*c)
  e=int((b-g)/30.6001)
  d=int(b-g-int(30.6001*e)+f)
  if e<14:
    m=e-1
  else:
    m=e-13
  if m>2:
    y=c-4716
  else:
    y=c-4715
  return [m,d,y]
```

```python
m=int(input("Month (1-12): "))
d=int(input("Day (1-31): "))
y=int(input("Year (1582-4000): "))
n=int(input("Number of days: "))
m,d,y=mdy(jd(m,d,y)+n)
print("{0}/{1}/{2}".format(m,d,y))
```

julian.py

This program demonstrates two functions that are very useful for a variety of calendar calculations. All other programs in this chapter use one or both of these functions.

jd() calculates the Julian Day Number for a given date in the year range 1582 to 4000. This is an absolute day number used by astronomers and others to clearly designate the sequence for each day, without regard to leap years and other such complications.

Note that for historical reasons, each astronomical day begins at noon Greenwich time, so there's an extra ".5" on these Julian Day Numbers. In the programs presented here we add and subtract whole days to find relative dates, and this extra fractional part doesn't really matter. For astronomical calculations this fractional part does become important.

The mdy() function provides a way to convert a Julian Day Number back to a triplet of numbers for the month, day, and year for that date. This makes it easy to add and subtract days to get a new date accurately, without having to do any complicated adjustments for the number of days in each month, or for leap years.

The example code inputs a date and outputs its Julian Day Number. Next, any Julian Day Number is input and the calendar date for that day is output. As shown, July 20, 1969 has Julian Day Number 2,440,422.5 and Julian Day Number 2,450,000.5 falls on October 10, 1995.

```
>>> from julian import *
Month (1-12): 7
Day (1-31): 20
Year (1582-4000): 1969
Julian Day:  2440422.5
Julian Day: 2450000.5
10/10/1995
>>>
```

```python
# julian.py
from math import *

def jd(m,d,y):
    if m<3:
        y-=1
        m+=12
    a=int(y/100)
    b=2-a+int(a/4)
    e=int(365.25*(y+4716))
    f=int(30.6001*(m+1))
    return b+d+e+f-1524.5

def mdy(jd):
    z=int(jd+.5)
    f=jd+.5-z
    if z<2299161:
        a=z
    else:
        t=int((z-1867216.25)/36524.25)
        a=z+1+t-int(t/4)
    b=a+1524
    c=int((b-122.1)/365.25)
    g=int(365.25*c)
    e=int((b-g)/30.6001)
    d=int(b-g-int(30.6001*e)+f)
    if e<14:
        m=e-1
    else:
        m=e-13
    if m>2:
        y=c-4716
    else:
        y=c-4715
    return [m,d,y]
```

```
m=int(input("Month (1-12): "))
d=int(input("Day (1-31): "))
y=int(input("Year (1582-4000): "))
j=jd(m,d,y)
print("Julian Day: ",j)
j=float(input("Julian Day: "))
m,d,y=mdy(j)
print("{0}/{1}/{2}".format(m,d,y))
```

two-days.py

How many days will you have been on the Earth on your next birthday? This kind of question is easy to answer with this program. Two dates are input, they are converted to Julian Day Numbers, and the difference between is output as the number of days between the two dates.

The jd() function is at the core of this program, and it is described in more detail elsewhere in this chapter.

The sample calculation finds the number of days from the day men landed on the Moon (July 20, 1969) and the date of Y2K, or January 1, 2000.

```
>>> from two_days import *

First date
Month (1-12): 7
Day (1-31): 20
Year (1582-4000): 1969

Second date
Month (1-12): 1
Day (1-31): 1
Year (1582-4000): 2000
```

```
Day (1-31): 20
Year (1582-4000): 1969

Second date
Month (1-12): 1
Day (1-31): 1
Year (1582-4000): 2000

7/20/1969
1/1/2000
Days between:   11122
>>>
```

```python
# two_days
def jd(m,d,y):
    if m<3:
        y-=1
        m+=12
    a=int(y/100)
    b=2-a+int(a/4)
    e=int(365.25*(y+4716))
    f=int(30.6001*(m+1))
    return b+d+e+f-1524.5

print("\nFirst date")
m1=int(input("Month (1-12): "))
d1=int(input("Day (1-31): "))
y1=int(input("Year (1582-4000): "))
print("\nSecond date")
m2=int(input("Month (1-12): "))
d2=int(input("Day (1-31): "))
y2=int(input("Year (1582-4000): "))
nd=int(abs(jd(m1,d1,y1)-jd(m2,d2,y2)))
print("\n{}/{}/{}".format(m1,d1,y1))
print("{}/{}/{}".format(m2,d2,y2))
print("Days between: ",nd)
```

3.

Electronics

This chapter presents a sampling of useful programs for doing various electronics calculations. The author has used these and similar calculations when inventing some fun gadgets, such as a bicycle brake light that requires no wiring, you just stick it on your bike or helmet and ride! It uses an accelerometer and some fun program code to get rid of bumps and rotations while detecting braking and putting on a bright brake light. (LucidBrakes™)

Whether you are experimenting with Arduino's, Raspberry Pi's, or creating your own circuits at the component level, these calculations can come in very handy.

ac_voltages.py

Homes in the United States are supplied with electrical power in the form of a sine wave with an effective voltage of about 117 volts. This effective voltage provides the same power in watts to a resistive load as would a DC voltage of 117 volts. Effective voltage is also called RMS, which stands for "Root-Mean-Squared", because of the way it is mathematically derived.

Most of the time we use the effective voltage value, because it is the value that allows quick calculation of power to a circuit. But there are two other ways to measure a sine wave voltage. The peak voltage, at the very top point of the sine wave, provides a "Peak" voltage value, and the average magnitude of the voltage over time, without regard to polarity, provides the "Average" voltage value.

Here are the two main conversion equations. All the relationships between Peak, Average, and RMS voltages can be figured out by algebraically working with these two:

$$V_{Peak} = V_{RMS} \times \sqrt{2}$$

$$V_{Peak} = V_{Average} \times \frac{\pi}{2}$$

This program provides the conversions between these three ways to describe a pure sine wave voltage. Enter the one known value when prompted for it, and just press "OK" to skip the other two. The program determines which value you've entered, calculates the other two, and outputs all three for easy reference.

```
# ac_voltages.py
from math import *

def ac_voltages(avg,peak,rms):
  if avg:
    peak=pi*avg/2
    rms=peak/sqrt(2)
  elif peak:
    avg=peak*2/pi
    rms=peak/sqrt(2)
  elif rms:
    peak=rms*sqrt(2)
    avg=peak*2/pi
  return [avg,peak,rms]

print("\n\nInput the one known value\n")
s=input("AC average voltage: ")
avg=float(s) if s else 0
s=input("AC peak voltage: ")
peak=float(s) if s else 0
s=input("AC RMS voltage: ")
rms=float(s) if s else 0
avg,peak,rms=ac_voltages(avg,peak,rms)
print("\nAvg: ",avg)
print("Peak: ",peak)
print("RMS: ",rms)
```

As shown in this sample run, a standard U.S. house wiring voltage of 117 V (RMS) has a peak voltage of about 165 V, and an average voltage over time of about 105 V.

```
Input the one known value

AC average voltage:
AC peak voltage:
AC RMS voltage: 117

Avg:   105.3370089903814
Peak:  165.4629867976521
RMS:   117.0
>>>
```

bridge.py

Balanced bridge circuits, also called Wheatstone bridges, are used in electronics for precision measurements and for other purposes. A common calculation is to find the value of one leg of a balanced bridge when the other three legs are known. For example, in the following figure we can calculate a value for R4 when R1, R2, and R3 are known. These values cause the ammeter across the middle to read zero amps. Similarly, a voltmeter across these same two nodes would read zero volts.

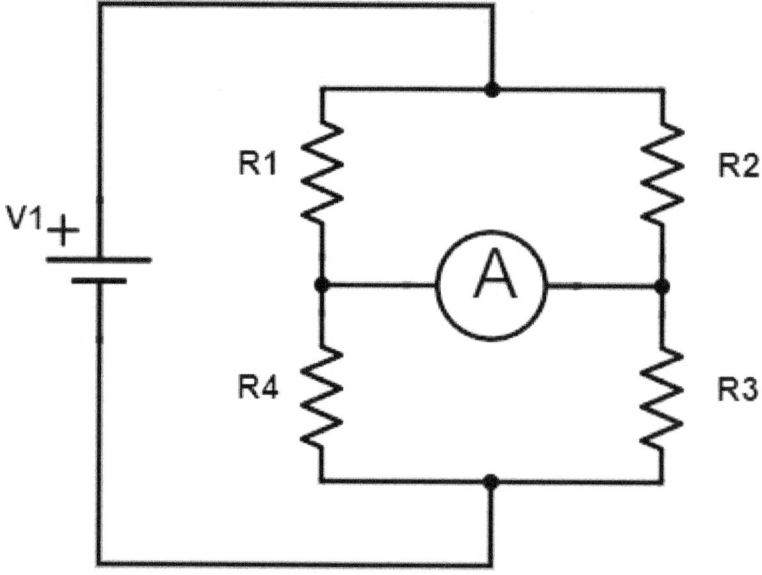

Here's the equation relating the four resistors:

$$R1 \times R3 = R2 \times R4$$

Note that the bridge() function uses variables z1 to z3 instead of R1 to R3. This is because of an awesome feature of NumWorks Python, where a variable can just as easily contain a complex number as it can a real number. In circuit analysis, complex numbers are very useful for AC circuits containing capacitors and inductors in addition to resistors. And yes, AC bridge circuits do follow all the same math rules when working with these components, using complex numbers for their respective impedances

The following example calculates the value of the 4th leg resistance when the first three resistors are 2700, 3900, and 5600 ohms, and it solves a second time for complex impedances of 4+3j, 5+0j, and 3-7j.

```
# bridge.py
def bridge(z1,z2,z3):
    return z1*z3/z2

r1=2700
r2=3900   # opposite the unknown
r3=5600
r4=bridge(r1,r2,r3)
print("r4: ",r4)

z1=4+3j
z2=5+0j   # opposite the unknown
z3=3-7j
z4=bridge(z1,z2,z3)
print("z4: ",z4)
```

The bridge() function is very small, just the first two lines of code. Most of this program demonstrates calling the bridge() function twice, once to solve for a pure resistive bridge, and a second time to balance a bridge composed of complex value impedances.

```
>>> from bridge import *
r4:   3876.923076923077
z4:   (6.6-3.8j)
>>>
```

As shown, the 4th resistor in the first case should be approximately 3877 ohms, and the impedance in the second case should be 6.6-3.8j ohms.

freq_wave.py

The electromagnetic spectrum covers a wide range of phenomena, such as radio waves, x-rays, visible light, infra-red light, microwaves, and so on. Each of these features falls into a band of frequencies, each frequency has a specific wavelength, and they all travel in free space at the speed of light.

Frequency in Hertz and Wavelength in meters are the exact inverse of each other. They are both a function of the speed of light. Here's the simplest equation that ties all this together, where C is the speed of light:

$$C = 299.792.458 \; m/s$$

$$C = Wavelength \times Frequency$$

Most of the time, wavelength and frequency are expressed in engineering notation, where the power of ten is a multiple of three. This notation converts easily to prefixes such as kilo, Mega, nano, and others, making it easier to grasp the magnitude of the value. The first function in this program, named eng(), formats numbers into engineering notation with any desired number of significant digits. You might want to isolate this function into a module for use in other programs you create.

This program prompts for a frequency, then for a wavelength if you skip entering a value for frequency. The unknown value in either case is calculated, both values are formatted into engineering notation, and the results are output to your NumWorks display.

Two example runs are shown, the first where a frequency is the known, and second where a wavelength is the known value.

```python
#freq_wave
from math import *

def eng(x,d):
  x=abs(x)
  if x==0:
    return "0.0"
  exp=floor(log10(x))
  mant=x/10**exp
  r = round(mant,d-1)
  x = r*pow(10.0,exp)
  p = int(floor(log10(x)))
  p3 = p//3
  value=x/pow(10.0,3*p3)
  s="{:f}".format(value)
  if s[d]!=".":
    s=s[0:d+1]
  else:
    s=s[0:d]
  if p3!=0:
    return "{}e{:d}".format(s,3*p3)
  else:
    return "{}".format(s)

c,f,w=299792458,0,0
print("\nEnter known value...")
f=input("Frequency: ")
f=float(f) if f else 0
```

```
if f==0:
  w=input("Wavelength (m): ")
  w=float(w) if w else 0
if w!=0:
  f=c/w
if f!=0:
  w=c/f
digits=5
print("\nFrequency:")
print("{} Hz".format(eng(f,digits)))
print("\nWavelength:")
print("{} meters".format(eng(w,digits)))
```

```
>>> from freq_wave import *

Enter known value...
Frequency: 3.1416

Frequency:
3.1416 Hz

Wavelength:
95.427e6 meters
>>>
```

```
>>> from freq_wave import *

Enter known value...
Frequency:
Wavelength (m): 1e8

Frequency:
2.9979 Hz

Wavelength:
100.00e6 meters
>>>
```

The variable named *digits*, near the end of the program, is set to five. Change this value if you want higher or lower precision in your answers.

For easy reference, here's a list of the metric prefixes for the various engineering notation powers of ten:

Y	$Yotta$	10^{24}		y	$yocto$	10^{-24}
Z	$Zetta$	10^{21}		z	$zepto$	10^{-21}
E	Exa	10^{18}		a	$atto$	10^{-18}
P	$Peta$	10^{15}		f	$femto$	10^{-15}
T	$Tera$	10^{12}		p	$pico$	10^{-12}
G	$Giga$	10^{9}		n	$nano$	10^{-9}
M	$Mega$	10^{6}		μ	$micro$	10^{-6}
k	$kilo$	10^{3}		m	$milli$	10^{-3}

led_resistor.py

LEDs are awesome. Once you know how to power them properly, you can light up all kinds of fun artwork, gadgets, and inventions in any color and blinking patterns imaginable. For example, the author invented a brake light for bicycles that requires no wiring to the brakes at all, instead relying on an accelerometer chip to determine when to flash bright red LEDs to indicate deceleration. Check out LucidBrakes™ online.

An LED is a special type of diode, where current flows easily in one direction through it, and not in the other direction. To light up an LED you need to use a resistor to limit the amount of current allowed to flow in the "easy" direction. This program helps you calculate the size of that resistor. It also helps determine the current and power requirements, to make sure no magic smoke is emitted from anything!

The standard way to wire up an LED is with a resistor in series, and a voltage source powering them both:

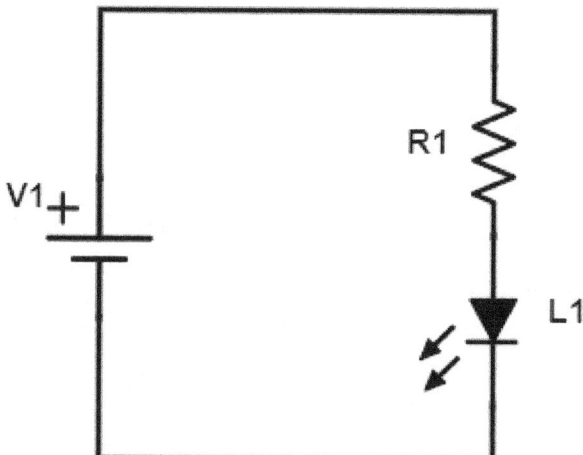

Here are the equations that tie together all the calculations we'll need in the program, where V_s is the source voltage, V_f is the forward voltage across the LED, V_r is the voltage across the resistor, i is is the current in amps through everything, W_r is the watts of power in the resistor, and W_f is the watts of power in the LED.

$$V_s = V_r + V_f$$
$$V_r = R \times i$$
$$W_r = i \times V_r$$
$$W_f = i \times V_f$$

Here's the the program listing:

```python
# led_resistor.py
def led_resistor(Vs,Vf,i):
    r=(Vs-Vf)/i
    Rw=(Vs-Vf)*i
    Lw=Vf*i
    return [r,Rw,Lw]

def led_current(Vs,Vf,r):
    i=(Vs-Vf)/r
    Rw=(Vs-Vf)*i
    Lw=Vf*i
    return [i,Rw,Lw]

Vs=float(input("\nSource Vs: "))
Vf=float(input("LED Vf: "))
print("\nNow enter one of these...")
i=input("Current in amps: ")
i=float(i) if i else 0
r=input("LED resistor in ohms: ")
r=float(r) if r else 0
if i:
    r,Rw,Lw=led_resistor(Vs,Vf,i)
else:
    i,Rw,Lw=led_current(Vs,Vf,r)
print("\nVs: ",Vs)
print("Vf: ",Vf)
print("R: {} ohms".format(r))
print("i: {} amps".format(i))
print("Rw: {} watts".format(Rw))
print("Lw: {} watts".format(Lw))
```

The following two example runs first find the approximate value for a resistor when the current is known, and the second example calculates the current when a standard resistor is selected for the circuit.

In both cases you enter the source voltage and the LED forward voltage (this Vf varies for LED types), and then either the current in amps or the resistor value in ohms.

```
>>> from led_resistor import ›

Source Vs: 9
LED Vf: 2.3

Now enter one of these...
Current in amps: .025
LED resistor in ohms: |
```

```
Now enter one of these...
Current in amps: .025
LED resistor in ohms:

Vs:  9.0
Vf:  2.3
R: 268.0 ohms
i: 0.025 amps
Rw: 0.1675 watts
Lw: 0.0575 watts
>>> |
```

For 25 mA of current, the approximate resistor size is calculated to be 268 ohms. The next run then inputs a standard resistor value of 270 ohms, and the current is then calculated to be about 24.8 milliamps.

```
>>> from led_resistor import ›

Source Vs: 9
LED Vf: 2.3

Now enter one of these...
Current in amps:
LED resistor in ohms: 270
```

```
Now enter one of these...
Current in amps:
LED resistor in ohms: 270

Vs:  9.0
Vf:  2.3
R:   270.0 ohms
i:   0.0248148148148148 amps
Rw:  0.1662592592592592 watts
Lw:  0.05707407407407406 watts
>>>
```

It's important not to burn out the resistor or the LED in your circuit. Resistors have a stated wattage, and they'll be okay if Rw is less than this value. In our example the resistor is heated with about 0.16 watts of power, so a standard quarter watt (0.25 watts) resistor should work fine. LEDs have a stated maximum current, which you can also check with these results.

ohms_laws.py

The subject of electricity and electronics is full of equations and formulas, but by far the two most important equations are what we call "Ohm's Laws". If you learn only how to work with the following two simple equations, you'll know enough to be considered an electronics whiz by most everyone you know.

$$E = I \times R$$
$$P = I \times E$$

The first equation states that voltage (Electromagnetic force) is equal to current in amps (I) times resistance in ohms (R). The second equation states that wattage (Power) is equal to current in amps times voltage.

It's easy to algebraically rearrange these two equations to calculate the unknowns when any two values are known. This program prompts you to enter any two of these four values, the other two quantities will be calculated, and all four values will be output.

For example, a 60 watt light bulb powered by standard household 117 volts uses a current of about half an amp, and it has a resistance of about 228 ohms, as shown.

```
Input two known values

Power in watts: 60
Current in amps:
Emf in volts: 117
Resistance in ohms:

Watts:   60.0
Amps:    0.5128205128205128
Volts:   117.0
Ohms:    228.15
>>>
```

The program prompts for each of the four values. Enter any two of them, and just press OK for the other two. All four values are displayed.

```python
# ohms_laws.py
def ohms_laws(p,i,e,r):
  if p and i:
    e=p/i
    r=p/(i*i)
  elif p and e:
    i=p/e
    r=(e*e)/p
  elif p and r:
    i=math.sqrt(p/r)
    e=math.sqrt(p*r)
  elif i and e:
    p=i*e
    r=e/i
  elif i and r:
    p=i*i*r
    e=i*r
  elif e and r:
    p=(e*e)/r
    i=e/r
  else:
    pass
  return ([p,i,e,r])
```

```
print("\n\nInput two known values\n")
p=input("Power in watts: ")
p=float(p) if p else 0
i=input("Current in amps: ")
i=float(i) if i else 0
e=input("Emf in volts: ")
e=float(e) if e else 0
r=input("Resistance in ohms: ")
r=float(r) if r else 0
p,i,e,r=ohms_laws(p,i,e,r)
print("\nWatts: ", p)
print("Amps: ", i)
print("Volts: ", e)
print("Ohms: ", r)
```

rc_timing.py

Many common timing circuits are based on an R-C charging configuration, the basics of which are shown here:

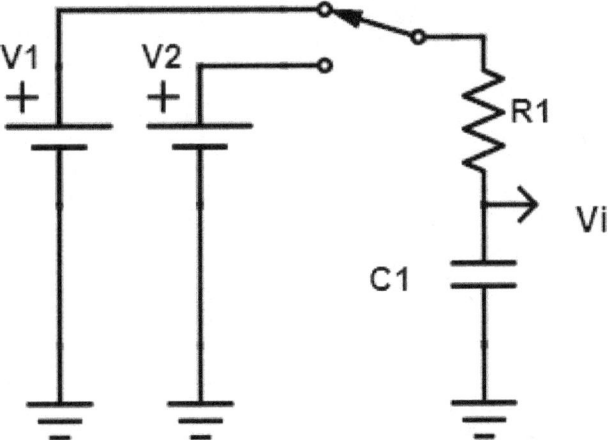

Capacitor C1 starts out with a voltage at Vi the same as V1. This starting voltage V1 is often zero, but it can be any voltage. When the input voltage switches to some other voltage V2, the capacitor starts to charge up as current flows into (or out of) it through R1. It takes time for the voltage at Vi to ramp up (or down) all the way to V2, and the details of this charging time is what this program is all about.

There are six variables in this calculation; the starting applied voltage V1, the new applied voltage V2, the instantaneous voltage Vi, the number of seconds S since the applied voltage was changed, and the values for resistance R and capacitance C that determine the changing rate of the instantaneous voltage. The bigger the resistor, the slower the capacitor will charge. The greater the difference between the two input voltages the faster the voltage across the capacitor will change. And so on. Here is the equation that relates all these parameters:

$$V_2 - V_i = (V_2 - V_1) \times e^{\frac{-S}{R \times C}}$$

This program algebraically isolates each variable in this equation to find its value when all the other variables are known. You are prompted to enter any five of the values, skipping the one unknown by just pressing EXE or OK. The unknown is calculated and all six values are output for easy reference.

```python
# rc_timing.py
from math import *

def rc_timing(v1,v2,vi,cap,res,sec):
  if not v1:
    tmp=exp(-sec/res/cap)
    v1=(vi+v2*(tmp-1))/tmp
  elif not v2:
    tmp=exp(-sec/res/cap)
    v2=(tmp*v1-vi)/(tmp-1)
  elif not vi:
    tmp=exp(-sec/res/cap)
    vi=v2-tmp*(v2-v1)
  elif not cap:
    tmp=-log((v2-vi)/(v2-v1))
    cap=sec/res/tmp
  elif not res:
    tmp=-log((v2-vi)/(v2-v1))
    res=sec/cap/tmp
  elif not sec:
    tmp=-log((v2-vi)/(v2-v1))
    sec=tmp*res*cap
  return [v1,v2,vi,cap,res,sec]

print("\nv1, v2, vi, cap, res, sec")
print("\nEnter all except for unknown")
v1=input("v1: ")
v1=1e-99 if v1=='0' else float(v1) if v1 else 0
v2=input("v2: ")
v2=1e-99 if v2=='0' else float(v2) if v2 else 0
vi=input("vi: ")
vi=1e-99 if vi=='0' else float(vi) if vi else 0
cap=input("cap: ")
cap=1e-99 if cap=='0' else float(cap) if cap else 0
res=input("res: ")
res=1e-99 if res=='0' else float(res) if res else 0
sec=input("sec: ")
sec=1e-99 if sec=='0' else float(sec) if sec else 0
v1,v2,vi,cap,res,sec=rc_timing(v1,v2,vi,cap,res,sec)
print("\nv1: ",v1)
print("v2: ",v2)
print("vi: ",vi)
print("cap: ",cap)
print("res: ",res)
print("sec: ",sec)
```

In our example run of this program we find how long it takes for a capacitor's voltage to rise from 0 to 4 volts after 5 volts is applied across a 47K ohm resistor. The capacitor is 6.8 microFarad. The first display image shows all the data entered, except for the unknown number of seconds:

```
>>> from rc_timing import *

v1, v2, vi, cap, res, sec

Enter all except for unknown
v1: 0
v2: 5
vi: 4
cap: 6.8e-6
res: 47e3
sec:
```

Immediately after pressing EXE the following display shows that the voltage across the capacitor will reach 4 volts after just slightly more than half a second.

```
vi: 4
cap: 6.8e-6
res: 47e3
sec:

v1:   1e-99
v2:   5.0
vi:   4.0
cap:  6.800000000000001e-06
res:  47000.0
sec:  0.5143763568139384
>>>
```

z_delta.py

This program converts resistances in a wye configuration to an equivalent delta configuration. The calculation also works for complex number impedances, as shown in the second example.

The delta configuration is called that because the three resistors are arranged in a triangle, although circuit diagrams often show them in more of a pi arrangement, as shown here. Notice that if you "pull together" the bottoms of RB and RC, a triangle is formed.

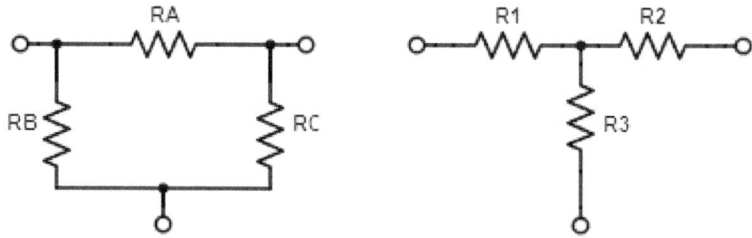

Similarly, the wye configuration is often shown as more of a "T" arrangement, as shown here. Just imagine the center point between R1, R2, and R3 pulled down a bit and you'll see the "Y", or wye shape.

The program uses the following equations to find values for RA, RB, and RC that form an equivalent set of resistances, or impedances, when given R1, R2, and R3.

$$RA = \frac{R1 \cdot R2 + R1 \cdot R3 + R2 \cdot R3}{R1}$$

$$RB = \frac{R1 \cdot R2 + R1 \cdot R3 + R2 \cdot R3}{R2}$$

$$RC = \frac{R1 \cdot R2 + R1 \cdot R3 + R2 \cdot R3}{R3}$$

The first three lines of code in the program define the function that does all the conversions from wye to delta. You can call this function by typing its name and passing parameters directly from the keyboard, or you can edit the values in the rest of the program listing, where the function is demonstrated. As shown, when you run the program the function is called twice, once with resistance values, and the second time with complex number impedances.

Three values, each either real or complex, are passed to the z_delta() function, and three values are returned. When a function returns multiple comma-separated-values, as in this program, Python packs the values into a tuple, and at the place where called from, the tuple is automatically unpacked into a set of comma-separated-variables. Python is awesome! To see all the output from the sample run, scroll the display on your calculator.

```
# z_delta
def z_delta(z1,z2,z3):
    tmp=z1*z2+z2*z3+z3*z1
    return tmp/z1,tmp/z2,tmp/z3

r1=300
r2=200
r3=400
ra,rb,rc=z_delta(r1,r2,r3)
print("\nr wye")
print(r1)
print(r2)
print(r3)
print("\nr delta")
print(ra)
print(rb)
print(rc)

z1=300+400j
z2=200-350j
z3=400+100j
za,zb,zc=z_delta(z1,z2,z3)
print("\nz wye")
print(z1)
print(z2)
print(z3)
print("\nz delta")
print(za)
print(zb)
print(zc)
```

```
650.0

z wye
(300+400j)
(200-350j)
(400+100j)

z delta
(546-578j)
(389.2307692307693+906.153846:
(955.8823529411764-126.470588:
>>>
```

z_parallel

Resistors in parallel can be replaced with a single equivalent resistor, a technique often used in circuit analysis. The same equation works for impedances in parallel too, so this one program works for resistances or impedances alike.

The equivalent resistance (or impedance) is calculated with the following formula:

$$\frac{1}{R_p} = \frac{1}{R1} + \frac{1}{R2} + \cdots + \frac{1}{Rn}$$

Here's a sketch showing how the multiple resistors are wired in parallel:

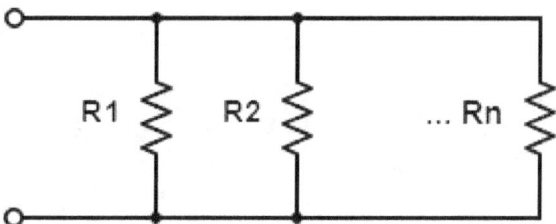

The example code first finds a single resistor equal to three resistors in parallel, and the second part repeats the calculation for three complex number impedances. The z_parallel() function does all the work, processing a list of values and returning a single equivalent value.

```
# z_parallel
def z_parallel(zlist):
   zp=sum(1/z for z in zlist)
   return 1/zp

r1=300
r2=200
r3=300
rp=z_parallel([r1,r2,r3])
print(rp)

z1=300+400j
z2=200-350j
z3=300+200j
zp=z_parallel([z1,z2,z3])
print(zp)
```

The two print() statements display the results for easy verification. In the first case, three resistors of 300, 200, and 300 ohms in parallel can be replaced with a resistance of about 85.7 ohms. In the second case, impedances with complex values of (300+400j), (200-350j), and (300+200j) can be replaced with components providing an impedance of about (202+42j). Here's the displayed results you should get:

```
>>> from z_parallel import *
85.71428571428571
(202.303961196443+42.0371867４
>>>
```

z_round

Numbers in Python are easily rounded to n decimal places using the round() function. Complex numbers, such as we are using for electrical impedance values in several programs in this book, are not so easily rounded. Look at the results displayed in the z_parallel program to see how the calculated complex number value is too long for the display line in NumWorks, requiring scrolling and mental rounding off to be useful.

The z_round function presented here rounds off each part of a complex number, and returns the simpler result. If you work with complex numbers often, you'll find this function useful.

```
# z_round
def z_round(z,n):
    r=round(z.real,n)
    i=round(z.imag,n)
    return r+i*1j

z1=(300+400j)**(1/3)
print(z1)
z2=z_round(z1,3)
print(z2)
```

The example code that calls the z_round() function creates a complex number with a full complement of decimal digits in both the real and imaginary parts by finding the cube root of (300+400j). The first line printed in the display shows part of this complex number. To see the whole thing you'll need to do some scrolling with the cursor. This number is then rounded to 3 decimal digits, for both the real and imaginary parts, and the result of (7.561+2.414j) is much easier to read and to work with, as shown in the second line of output.

```
>>> from z_round import *
(7.560856467169438+2.41443616:
(7.561+2.414j)
>>> 
```

z_series

Resistors in series can be replaced with a single resistor calculated as the sum of the resistances. Here's the formula:

$$Rs = R1 + R2 + \cdots + Rn$$

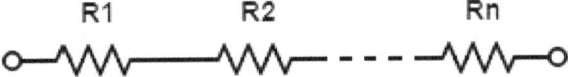

This formula is also valid for complex number impedances connected in series, and the sample code shows both a set of resistors and a set of impedances converted to equivalent single values by calling the z_series() function.

```
# z_series
def z_series(zlist):
    zs=sum(z for z in zlist)
    return zs

r1=250
r2=500
rs=z_series([r1,r2])
print(rs)

z1=300+400j
z2=200-350j
z3=300+200j
zs=z_series([z1,z2,z3])
print(zs)
```

```
>>> from z_series import *
750
(800+250j)
>>> 
```

z_wye.py

This program converts resistances in a delta configuration to an equivalent wye configuration. The calculation also works for complex number impedances, as shown in the second example.

The delta configuration is called that because the three resistors are arranged in a triangle, although circuit diagrams often show them in more of a pi arrangement, as shown here. Notice that if you "pull together" the bottoms of RB and RC, a triangle is formed.

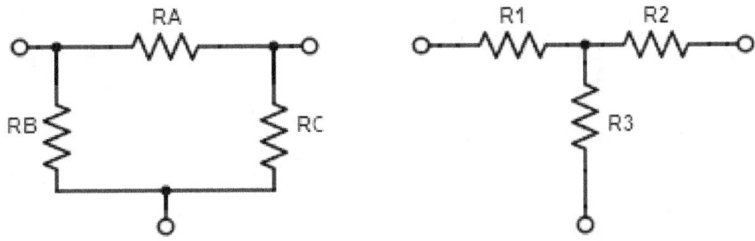

Similarly, the wye configuration is often shown as more of a "T" arrangement, as shown here. Just imagine the center point between R1, R2, and R3 pulled down a bit and you'll see the "Y", or wye shape.

The program uses the following equations to find values for R1, R2, and R3 that form an equivalent set of resistances, or impedances, when given RA, RB, and RC.

$$R1 = \frac{RB \cdot RC}{RA + RB + RC}$$

$$R2 = \frac{RA \cdot RC}{RA + RB + RC}$$

$$R3 = \frac{RA \cdot RB}{RA + RB + RC}$$

The first three lines of code in the program define the function that does all the conversions from delta to wye. You can call this function by typing its name and passing parameters directly from the keyboard, or you can edit the values in the rest of the program listing, where the function is demonstrated. As shown, when you run the program the function is called twice, once with resistance values, and the second time with complex number impedances.

Three values, each either real or complex, are passed to the z_wye() function, and three values are returned. To see all the output from the sample run, scroll the display on your calculator.

```
# z-wye
def z_wye(za,zb,zc):
    tmp=za+zb+zc
    return zb*zc/tmp,za*zc/tmp,za*zb/tmp

ra=867
rb=1300
rc=650
r1,r2,r3=z_wye(ra,rb,rc)
print("\nr delta")
print(ra)
print(rb)
print(rc)
print("\nr wye")
print(r1)
print(r2)
print(r3)

za=546-578j
zb=389+906j
zc=956-126j
z1,z2,z3=z_wye(za,zb,zc)
print("\nz delta")
print(za)
print(zb)
print(zc)
print("\nz wye")
print(z1)
print(z2)
print(z3)
```

```
400.1064962726304

z delta
(546-578j)
(389+906j)
(956-126j)

z wye
(299.7663009081521+400.08948O:
(200.1344712077496-349.968858
(399.9241598314479+99.973199:
>>>
```

4.

Games and Chance

This chapter lets you explore some fascinating statistics and probability challenges, as well as play some stimulating games.

Have you ever heard of the Monty Hall puzzle? This one has stumped some of the best minds in the world, but it's easy to create a NumWorks program to test out the correct answer. Be sure to take a close look at that program.

Other programs in this chapter include dealing a deck of cards, flipping coins millions of times, calculating the value of pi using darts and needles, and jumbling up words to see what you can find.

cards.py

This program creates a deck of standard playing cards, shuffles the deck, and then deals a hand of as many cards as you wish. The deck consists of 52 cards plus any number of joker cards desired.

At the heart of this program are two functions you might want to use in the creation of a more complicated card game. Call deck() to create a shuffled deck, and pass this deck (a Python list) to card() to deal cards with no repetition.

```
>>> from cards import *
How many jokers: 2
Deal how many cards: 7

Queen of Hearts
Ace of Hearts
Queen of Clubs
King of Clubs
Joker
2 of Hearts
10 of Diamonds
>>>
```

In this example a deck with two jokers is created and shuffled, and a hand of seven cards is dealt.

The randrange() function imported from the random module creates a different deck every time the program is run.

```
# cards.py
from random import *

def deck(j):
  d=list(range(52+j))
  for i in range(52+j):
    k=randrange(52+j)
    d[i],d[k]=d[k],d[i]
  return d

def card(d,n):
  c=d[n]
  if c>51:
    return "Joker"
  suit=["Hearts","Clubs","Spades","Diamonds"]
  face=["Ace","2","3","4","5","6","7","8",
      "9","10","Jack","Queen","King"]
  return face[c%13]+" of "+suit[c//13]

j=int(input("How many jokers: "))
d=deck(j)

n=int(input("Deal how many cards: "))
print("")
if n>len(d):
  msg="Deck has only {} cards"
  print(msg.format(len(d)))
else:
  for i in range(n):
    print(card(d,i))
```

coinflips.py

On the average, how many times do you need to flip a coin to get five heads in a row? This can be solved with an explicit mathematical formula, as shown in the last line of this program, but it's much more fun to have your NumWorks calculator simulate a whole bunch of flips in a row to get an approximate answer. The more times you flip the coin, the more accurate the answer gets, on the average of course. This is a good example of a Monte Carlo simulation, where a lot of random trials can be run in a computer to get closer and closer to an accurate real-world answer.

In this case, it is predicted mathematically that it takes an average of 62 flips of a coin in a row to get five heads in a row. Some times less, some times more, but on the average it works out to 62 flips.

```
>>> from coinflips import *

Flips to get 5 heads in a row
Trials:   100
Average:   57.19
Predicted:   62
>>>
```

The program uses the random library to generate random flips of a coin, counting up every time a head shows up, resetting the count when a tail shows up, and stopping each trial when five heads in a row finally show up. As shown, after 100 trials, it took an average of 57.19 flips to get five heads in a row. Run this program several times to see this average shift to values in the neighborhood of 62.

Feel free to experiment by changing the number of trials, or the target number of heads in a row. Be careful though, as the program can take a long time to run if larger numbers are used.

```python
# coinflips.py
from random import *

goal=5
trials=100
tally=0

def flips():
  n=0
  inarow=0
  while 1:
    n+=1
    if randint(0,1):
      inarow+=1
    else:
      inarow=0
    if inarow==goal:
      return n

for i in range(trials):
  tally+=flips()

print("")
print("Flips to get",goal,"heads in a row")
print("Trials: ",trials)
print("Average: ",tally/trials)
print("Predicted: ",2**(goal+1)-2)
```

dice.py

This program rolls a handful of six-sided dice, showing the numbers on each of them, their sum, and their average.

```
>>> from dice import *

How many dice: 2
2 2
Sum: 4  Avg: 2.0

How many dice: 4
3 3 6 2
Sum: 14  Avg: 3.5

How many dice:
```

In this example the first roll uses two dice, and the second roll throws four of them.

An interesting challenge would be to modify this program to throw a standard set of dice for Dungeons and Dragons. You'll need one each of 4, 6, 8, 10, 12, and 20 sided dice.

```python
# dice.py
from random import *

while 1:
  try:
    n=int(input("\nHow many dice: "))
    s=""
    t=0
    for i in range(n):
      d=randint(1,6)
      t+=d
      s+=str(d)+" "
    print(s)
    print("Sum: {}  Avg: {}".format(t,t/n))
  except:
    break
```

digits.py

Digits.py is a challenging game that can be a lot of fun, or it can drive you nuts! It definitely will stretch your brain cells as you up your level. Level 1 is ridiculously easy, and yet I don't know anyone who has solved a level 9 game at this time. Maybe you will be the first!

The rules are fairly simple. The digits 1 to 9 are arranged at random in a 3 x 3 grid, with a few of them missing. You need to figure out what the missing digits are. Around the edges of the game are clue numbers. They're located at the ends of each row and column, and they are the result of secretly adding or subtracting the digits in the given row or column.

Start with skill level 1. This will create a very simple game that helps you understand how the game is played. Here we go:

```
DIGITS - an add/sub game

Place the digits 1 thru 9 in
center. Add or subtract along
each row/col to match results.
(Scroll up to see solution)


Enter level 1 to 9...
1 Beginner
9 Ultra Wizard
? 1
```

Enter a 1 to choose the simplest level. Here's an example of what shows:

```
 deg              PYTHON



            7  -6   0

       3    5   _   7   7
       11   6   1   4   1
       -7   8   2   3   9

            19  6   0



 >>> |
```

Notice that the middle area has all the digits 1 through 9, except for the digit 9. It's obvious that the underscored spot is where the 9 goes. Now look at the top of that column. The digits in that column, 2, 1 and 9, can add and subtract to get a result of -6. Add 2 plus 1 and subtract 9. The 6 at the bottom of that column can be calculated as 9 - 1 - 2. Similarly, the 7 at the right end of that row is calculated as 5 + 9 - 7. Your challenge is to find each digit's location using the plus or minus signs randomly used such that the answers at the ends of each row and column can work correctly.

Okay, that was easy. Now set the level to something like 5:

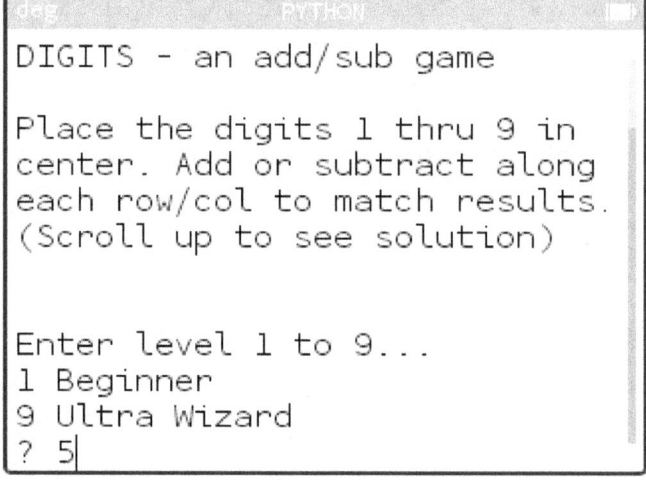

This creates a much more challenging puzzle to be solved:

```
deg                    PYTHON

                6    13    2

          7     3     4    _    5
          8     _     2    1    8
         -6     _     _    _   24

                6    -1   14


>>>
```

The digits 1 to 4 are visible, and the digits 5 through 9 are hidden. Take a look at the first row, where 3 plus or minus 4 plus or minus an unknown digit results in a value of 5. There are a couple of possible digits that might work, but 6 is the only missing digit we can place at this spot. How long will it take you to find where the rest of the digits must be placed?

If you get stuck, scroll up on your NumWorks display to see the arrangement of the 9 digits for the solution.

I suggest creating a level 9 game, writing down on paper the puzzle that shows, and then working on it off and on throughout the day. This is a good way, much like playing Sudoko, to keep your brain cells flexed and exercised in an interesting way. Can you find the solution faster than your friends?

```python
# digits.py
from random import *

def rsign():
    return randint(0,1) * 2 - 1

def add_sub(a,b,c):
    return a + rsign() * b + rsign() * c

def fmt(n,w):
    f="{:"+str(w)+"}"
    return f.format(n)
```

```
# Get desired challenge
print("\n\nDIGITS - an add/sub game\n")
print("Place the digits 1 thru 9 in")
print("center. Add or subtract along")
print("each row/col to match results.")
print("(Scroll up to see solution)\n")
print("\nEnter level 1 to 9...")
print("1 Beginner")
print("9 Ultra Wizard")
w=int(input("? "))

# Create and shuffle the digits
dg=[1,2,3,4,5,6,7,8,9]
for i in range(9):
  j=randint(0,8)
  dg[i],dg[j]=dg[j],dg[i]

# Create 12 edge values
ans = []
ans.append(add_sub(dg[6],dg[3],dg[0]))
ans.append(add_sub(dg[7],dg[4],dg[1]))
ans.append(add_sub(dg[8],dg[5],dg[2]))
ans.append(add_sub(dg[0],dg[1],dg[2]))
ans.append(add_sub(dg[3],dg[4],dg[5]))
ans.append(add_sub(dg[6],dg[7],dg[8]))
ans.append(add_sub(dg[2],dg[5],dg[8]))
ans.append(add_sub(dg[1],dg[4],dg[7]))
ans.append(add_sub(dg[0],dg[3],dg[6]))
ans.append(add_sub(dg[8],dg[7],dg[6]))
ans.append(add_sub(dg[5],dg[4],dg[3]))
ans.append(add_sub(dg[2],dg[1],dg[0]))
```

```python
# Create string layout
sp=" "

# Top row
s=sp*8
for i in range(3):
    s+=fmt(ans[i],3)+sp

# Three middle rows
k=0
s+="\n"
for i in range(3):
    s+="\n"+sp*3+fmt(ans[11-i],3)+sp*2
    for j in range(3):
        if dg[k] <=9-w:
            s+=sp*2+str(dg[k])+sp
        else:
            s+=sp*2+"_"+sp
        k+=1
    s+=fmt(ans[3+i],5)

# Bottom row
s+="\n\n"+sp*8
for i in range(3):
    s+=fmt(ans[8-i],3)+sp
s+="\n\n"

# Output solution
print("\n"*5)
print(dg[0],dg[1],dg[2])
print(dg[3],dg[4],dg[5])
print(dg[6],dg[7],dg[8])
print("\n"*30)

# Output the game
print(s)
```

hunt_dist.py

This program is a game that challenges your visual-spatial skills, as well as your numerical and analytic thinking processes. Plus, it's fun!

Somewhere in a 100 x 100 grid there's a critter/target/goal for you to find. You enter a coordinate pair, and the straight-line distance to the hidden spot is calculated and shown. The goal is to find the critter/target/goal in as few guesses as possible.

You might want to get a piece of graph paper and sketch circles centered on your guess points. This should allow you to find the target in just a few guesses, and it isn't cheating as long as you're having fun and learning something about the pythagorean theorem and other analytical geometry skills. Or, like me, you can just intuit your guesses, trying to shorten the distance with each guess, and reversing course when getting further away. That's fun too.

Here's a short sample run of the game (usually it can take more that 5 guesses), but it shows how things work:

```
x,y? 30,30
Dist:   42.29657196511321
x,y? 30,72
Dist:   63.0317380372777
x,y? 70,25
Dist:   2.0
x,y? 70,27
Dist:   2.82842712474619
x,y? 72,25

Bingo! at 5 guesses
>>>
```

Notice in the source code there's a commented out line, where it prints the target x and y values. Feel free to uncomment this line to make the game easier. You'll see the critter/target/goal coordinates and you can play around with the guesses to see how the distance works out with each guess.

```python
# hunt_dist.py
from random import *

x=randrange(100)
y=randrange(100)
# print(x,y)
n=0
while 1:
    n+=1
    g=input("x,y? ").split(",")
    a=int(g[0])
    b=int(g[1])
    d=((x-a)**2+(y-b)**2)**.5
    if d==0:break
    print("Dist: ",d)
print("\nBingo! at {} guesses".format(n))
```

hunt_news.py

Compared to hunt_dist, this game is exactly the same, only different (one of my favorite sayings.) Your goal is to find the randomly assigned target coordinate in a 100 x 100 grid. With each guess you are directed towards the target using map-like directions, such as "Move SE" for south-east, or "Move W" for straight west. The goal is to find the target in as few moves as possible.

Here's a sample run of the game. In this case I uncommented the print(x,y) line so you can see that the target is at 57,30. The coordinates use the bottom left corner as the origin, or x,y point of (0,0).

```
>>> from hunt_news import *
57 30
x,y? 50,50
Move SE
x,y? 60,20
Move NW
x,y? 57,30

Bingo! at 3 guesses
>>>
```

```python
# hunt_news.py
from random import *

x=randrange(100)
y=randrange(100)
#print(x,y)
n=0
while 1:
    n+=1
    g=input("x,y? ").split(",")
    a=int(g[0])
    b=int(g[1])
    d=""
    if b<y:d+="N"
    if b>y:d+="S"
    if a<x:d+="E"
    if a>x:d+="W"
    if d=="":break
    print("Move",d)
print("\nBingo! at {} guesses".format(n))
```

maze.py

This program uses the kandinsky graphics module to sketch a random maze on your NumWorks calculator. Every time you run the program, a different maze is drawn, so it's a new challenge every time.

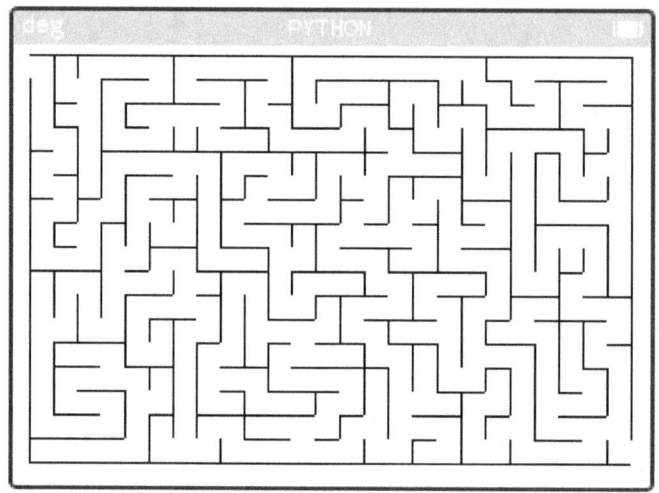

The art and science of creating mazes is very interesting. Check out the internet if this subject is of interest to you. Or, you can just have some fun by running this program to see how fast you can mentally navigate from the upper left corner to the bottom right to help keep your brain cells in good shape.

```python
# maze
from kandinsky import *
from random import *

def vline(x,y,w):
  if w:
    x1=x*wl+9
    y1=y*wl+5
    fill_rect(x1,y1,1,wl,color(0,0,0))
```

```python
def hline(x,y,w):
  if w:
    x1=x*wl+9
    y1=y*wl+5
    fill_rect(x1,y1,wl,1,color(0,0,0))

def cell(x,y):
  z=a[x+y*w]
  hline(x,y,z&1)
  vline(x+1,y,z&2)
  hline(x,y+1,z&4)
  vline(x,y,z&8)

def disp():
  for x in range(w):
    for y in range(h):
      cell(x,y)

def nor(u):
  v=u-w
  if v>0:
    if a[v]==15:
      a[u]&=14
      a[v]&=11
      return v
  return u
```

```
def eas(u):
  v=u+1
  if v%w:
    if a[v]==15:
      a[u]&=13
      a[v]&=7
      return v
  return u

def sou(u):
  v=u+w
  if v<n:
    if a[v]==15:
      a[u]&=11
      a[v]&=14
      return v
  return u

def wes(u):
  v=u-1
  if u%w:
    if a[v]==15:
      a[u]&=7
      a[v]&=13
      return v
  return u

def move(u):
  for i in range(c):
    d=randrange(4)
    if d==0:
      u=nor(u)
    if d==1:
      u=eas(u)
    if d==2:
      u=sou(u)
    if d==3:
      u=wes(u)
```

```
# Initialize
w=25
h=17
n=w*h
c=n/4
wl=12
a=[15 for x in range(n)]
t=[x for x in range(n)]
a[0]=7

while 1:

   # Shuffle the indexes
   for i in range(n):
      j=randrange(n)
      t[i],t[j]=t[j],t[i]

   # Check each cell in index order
   done=True
   for i in range(n):
      u=t[i]
      if a[u]==15:
         done=False
      else:
         move(u)

   # Done if all cells connected
   if done:
      break

# Done
a[n-1]&=13
disp()
```

memory.py

This game challenges your short term memory abilities. If you play it enough, it might help you in the long term. Don't forget that! Or if you do, perhaps you should play this game more often. Sorry, I get carried away sometimes.

Anyway, the way it works is that a short integer is displayed until you're ready to proceed. Press OK or EXE and the number will disappear. You are prompted to type the number in from memory, and if correct you get a longer number. If you don't enter the number correctly, a shorter number appears for the next guess. After a dozen number challenges your total score appears, as calculated from the total lengths of all the numbers.

Here's a sample of the game in progress. Note that you need to press OK or EXE to clear the screen before recalling and entering the number you just stared at.

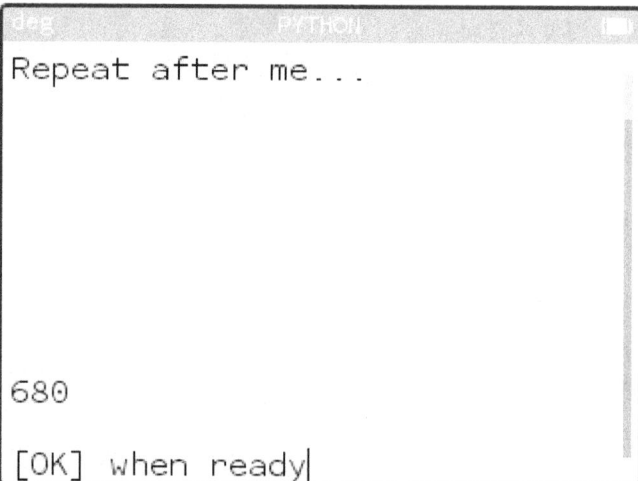

```
? 680
Yes!
11  guesses until final score




5219

[OK] when ready
```

```python
# Memory
from random import *

def digs(n):
  x=randint(1,9)
  for i in range(n-1):
    x=x*10+randrange(10)
  return x

n=0
s=3
t=0
print("\nRepeat after me...","\n"*6)
for i in range(12):
  n+=1
  t+=s
  x=digs(s)
  print("\n")
  print(x)
  try:
    z=input("\n[OK] when ready")
  except:
    z=0
```

```
    print("\n"*17)
    try:
      g=int(input("? "))
    except:
      g=0
    if g==x:
      print("Yes!")
      s+=1
    else:
      print("Sorry")
      s-=1
    msg=" guesses until final score"
    print(str(12-n),msg)
    print("\n"*3)
  print("\n\nFinal Score: ",t)
```

monty_hall.py

Have you heard of the famous Monty Hall puzzle? It's a doozy, and it baffled some top minds when it was first discussed.

So, Monty shows you three doors, and states there's a car behind one of them. You guess one of the doors. Before opening your door to see if you won, Monty opens one of the other two doors, where nothing is behind that door. Then he asks if you want to switch with the last door before the big reveal. Should you switch? Will it make any difference?

Many people say that since there are two unopened doors left, there's a fifty-fifty chance the car is behind either one. So it won't matter if you switch before Monty opens your door. But it turns out that is wrong!

This program performs a Monte Carlo simulation (this Monte is unrelated to the other Monty, or to the Full Monty for that matter, but that's another story.) The program simulates you being asked 1000 times by Monty if you want to switch, and it tallies the number of times you win the car if you do switch and if you don't switch.

If you do switch, your odds of winning are 2 times out of 3, and if you don't switch your odds are 1 out of 3. In summary, make that switch!

If this result baffles you, read up on the Internet about the "Monty Hall Problem", or watch any of the several Youtube videos that cover the subject. Meanwhile, have fun simulating a bunch of wins with your NumWorks calculator!

```
>>> from monty_hall import *

Win percent when contestant
does not swap last 2 doors:
32.4

Win percent when contestant
does swap last 2 doors:
65.2
>>>
```

```python
# monty_hall.py
from random import *

games=1000

for n in range(2):
  if n:
    switch=True
  else:
    switch=False
  wins=0
  for i in range(games):
    doors=[False,False,False]
    doors[randrange(3)]=True
    choice1=randrange(3)
    monty_opens=randrange(3)
    while True:
      monty_opens=randrange(3)
      if monty_opens==choice1:
        continue
      if doors[monty_opens]:
        continue
      break
    if switch==False:
      if doors[choice1]==True:
        wins+=1
    else:
      if doors[choice1]==False:
        wins+=1
  if switch:
    s="does"
  else:
    s="does not"
  print("\nWin percent when contestant")
  print("{} swap last 2 doors:".format(s))
  print(round(100*wins/games,2))
```

pi_buffon.py

The value of pi can be calculated in many ways, including simulating real-world randomness with random numbers. A guy named Georges-Louis de Buffon came up with a cool method along these lines, way back in the 18th century, way before the first NumWorks calculator was thought of. He suggested dropping needles randomly on a floor marked with parallel lines with fixed spacing, and counting the number of needles that touched one of the lines when it came to rest with the total number dropped.

There are many places on the Internet where you can read up on all the math involved in this process, all leading to an estimate of the value of pi. It really is ingenious. With your NumWorks calculator you can simulate dropping thousands of needles in just seconds, a good feature since this method really is slow to converge accurately on the value of pi. You'd have to have a lot of patience to use real needles!

The program asks how many needles you want to drop. Try 1,000 or perhaps 10,000 needles for reasonable run times. Try more if you can let your calculator sit on a shelf and run for a long time, or less if you just want to see some crude estimates of pi. Here's the result of choosing 10,000 needles:

```
>>> from pi_buffon import *
How many needles: 10000
3.145643284051589
>>> 
```

Similar programs for calculating pi using random numbers are pi_darts.py and pi_graphics.py.

```
# pi_buffon.py
from random import *
from math import *

def buffon(n):
  h=0
  p2=pi*2
  for i in range(n):
    x=random()
    a=uniform(0,p2)
    x2=x+cos(a)
    if x2<0 or x2>1:
      h+=1
  return 2.0*n/h

n=int(input("How many needles: "))
print(buffon(n))
```

pi_darts.py

Imagine a special dartboard that is square with a circle in it that just touches the square's edges.

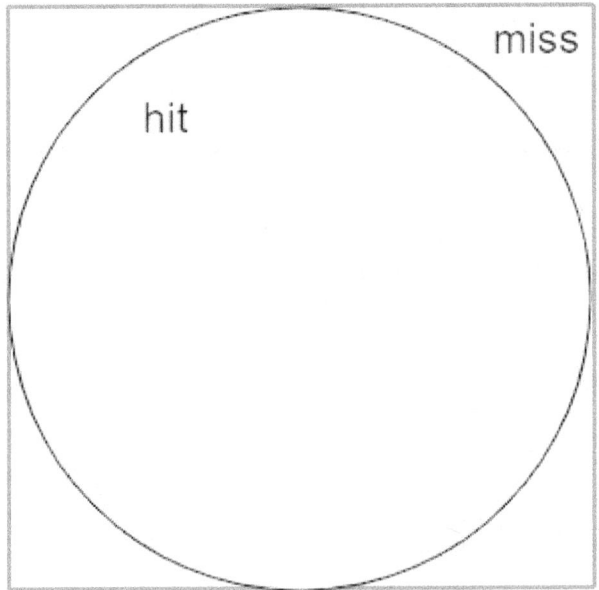

If you throw darts at this dartboard completely at random, so every square inch has just as much chance of getting hit as any other square inch, then the ratio of the number of hits in the circle to the number of total throws can provide an estimate of the value of pi. This is easy to see because the ratio is dependent on the areas of the circle and the square, and the area of the circle is calculated using the value of pi.

$$Area = \pi * r^2$$

This program is another example of a Monte Carlo simulation, where a lot of random trials provide an estimate of a value, in this case pi. Here's a sample simulation of throwing 10,000 darts:

```
>>> from pi_darts import *
How many darts: 10000
3.1348
>>>
```

Just like Buffon's needles, this is not a very efficient way to calculate or estimate the value of pi, it's just informative and fun to see how it works.

```
# pi_darts.py
from random import *

def pi(darts):
  h=0
  for i in range(darts):
    x=random()
    y=random()
    if x*x+y*y<1:
      h+=1
  return 4*h/darts

n=int(input("How many darts: "))
print(pi(n))
```

pi_graphics.py

This program extends the functionality of the pi_darts.py program by drawing the results of throwing lots of darts at a specially constructed simulated dart board. Notice that the program simplifies the dart board by effectively only using one corner of the previous dart board. This makes the math easier and faster. If the bottom left corner is at coordinate (0,0) and the top right corner is at (1,1) then simple and unmodified calls to random() will find values with equal distribution throughout the square.

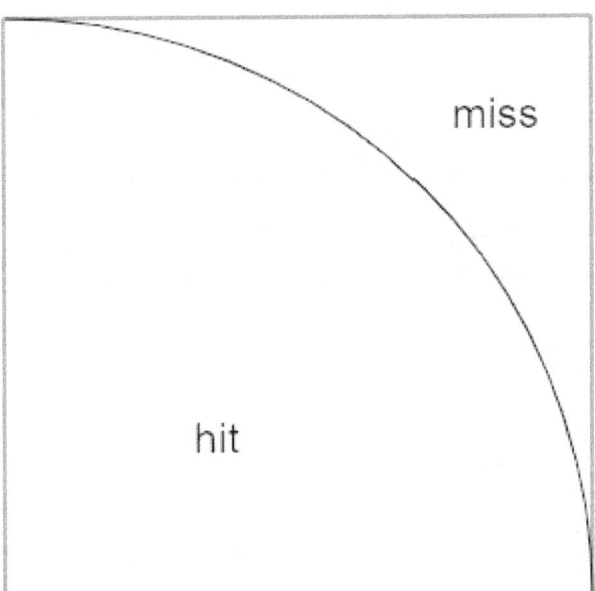

Once again, the ratio of the hits to the total number of darts thrown provides a way to estimate the value of pi. This program lets you see where all the darts landed, by sketching dots using the kandinsky set_pixel() function.

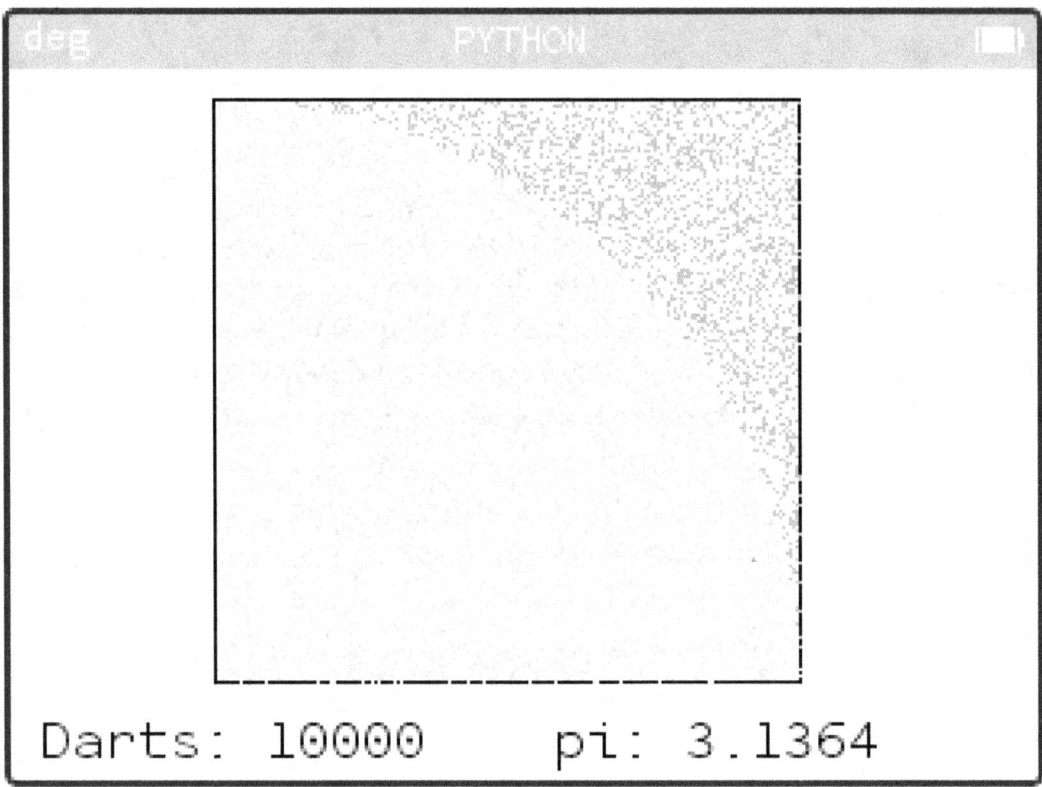

```python
# pi_graphics.py
from random import *
from kandinsky import *

def dot(x,y,c):
    xp=round(180*x+65)
    yp=round(180*(1-y)+10)
    set_pixel(xp,yp,c)

def pi(n):
    h=0
    for i in range(n):
        x=random()
        y=random()
        if x*x+y*y<1:
            h+=1
            dot(x,y,color(0,255,0))
        else:
            dot(x,y,color(255,0,0))
    return 4*h/n

n=int(input("How many darts: "))
black=(0,0,0)
gray=(234,234,234)
fill_rect(64,9,182,182,black)
fill_rect(65,10,180,180,color(255,255,255))
d="Darts: "+str(n)
p="pi: "+str(pi(n))
draw_string(d,10,200)
draw_string(p,170,200)
```

random_bytes.py

The random module provides several types of pseudorandom numbers. This program calls the getrandbits(8) function to generate random integers containing 8 bits. In other words, calling this function this way returns random bytes.

```
>>> from random_bytes import *
10000 127.2319
>>>
```

The program simply adds up all the random bytes and divides by the number of bytes. The average should be approximately 127.5. You might at first think the average should be 128, since a byte can hold 256 unique values in 8 bits. That is true, but those values run from 0 when no bits are set, up to 255 when all the bits are set to 1. The average of these values is 127.5.

The actual average calculated from 10,000 bytes won't be exactly 127.5, but if you run this program several times you should see averages that kind of average out to about 127.5. More or less.

```python
# random_bytes.py
from random import *

n=10000
x=0
for i in range(n):
    x+=getrandbits(8)
print(n,x/n)
```

word_jumble.py

This program asks for a word or phrase, then jumbles up the letters randomly as many times as you want. This is handy for various anagram or word jumble puzzles or challenges. For example, I entered my first and last name, nine letters in all, and asked for 5 random jumbles to be output:

```
>>> from word_jumble import *
Jumble word or phrase?
? john craig

How many jumbles? 5
JIHNCOARG
CNHJRAIGO
RAHNOGJCI
COJRHGAIN
RCHJAIGON

How many jumbles?
```

Already I started to see some short words, such as OR, AIR, HOG, HAIR, and so on. I continued to ask for 9 more jumbles (9 fills the screen nicely), and some bigger words started to pop into my mind as I stared at the results, words like CHAGRIN, CIGAR, JARGON, JOIN, and GAIN.

```
How many jumbles? 9
NGRAHJCOI
NACOJHIRG
IRHJGACNO
AIRJNCHGO
OHCNJAGIR
GOHJIRANC
OAIJRNHCG
HGANOCRJI
JOICHGRNA

How many jumbles?
```

You can keep on shuffling as many times as you want, and the program will end when you just press OK without entering a count.

```
# word_jumble.py
from random import *

print("Jumble word or phrase?")
s=input("? ")
s=list(s.replace(" ","").upper())
m=len(s)
while 1:
  try:
    n=int(input("\nHow many jumbles? "))
  except:
    break
  while n:
    n-=1
    for i in range(m):
      j=randrange(m)
      s[i],s[j]=s[j],s[i]
    t=""
    for i in range(m):
      t+=s[i]
    print(t)
```

word_perm.py

This program processes the letters in a word up to 5 characters in length, and displays all possible permutations, or rearrangements without repetition. For example, my first name, JOHN, can be arranged into 24 different combinations.

```
>>> from word_perm import *
Word? john
JOHN  JONH  JHON  JHNO  JNOH  JNHO
OJHN  OJNH  OHJN  OHNJ  ONJH  ONHJ
HJON  HJNO  HOJN  HONJ  HNJO  HNOJ
NJOH  NJHO  NOJH  NOHJ  NHJO  NHOJ

>>>
```

My last name, CRAIG, has five characters, and the permutations of its letters works out to 120 unique sequences. As you can see, the number of permutations increases rapidly as the length of a word increases. For N characters the number of permutations is N! (factorial). A six character word would have 720 combinations, so I limited the program to just five character words. You can change the code to allow more than 5 if you wish, just be prepared for a lot of output, and a lot of scrolling to see all the results!

```
# word_perm.py
def perm(s):
  if len(s)==1:
    return [s]
  b=[]
  for i in range(len(s)):
    m=s[i]
    c=s[:i]+s[i+1:]
    for j in perm(c):
      b.append(m+j)
  return b

while 1:
  s=input("Word? ")
  if len(s)>5:
    print("5 chars max\n")
  else:
    break
p=perm(s.upper())
u=""
for t in p:
  u+=t+" "
  if len(u)>25:
    print(u)
    u=""
print(u)
```

5.

GPS and Navigation

Latitudes and Longitudes are a lot of fun, especially when a high percentage of people now own smartphones with GPS chips that tell them exactly where they are at all times. Also, Google (and other) maps provide a great way to determine the location of any point on the Earth that you zoom in to.

This chapter lets you use such coordinates on the Earth's surface to calculate distances, directions, and even the land area defined by three or more coordinates.

These calculations are not as simple as distances, directions, and areas given cartesian coordinates in an x,y plane. This is because the Earth is a sphere, causing lines of longitude to be "squeezed together" the closer you get to the north or south poles. But your NumWorks calculator is very capable of working out all the math to get the job done.

area_gps.py

Finding an area on the surface of the Earth given several latitude and longitude coordinates at the corners of the area is more complicated than you might think. This program greatly simplifies the process.

The first complication occurs when finding the distance between any two GPS coordinates. The distance between lines of longitude, that is how far east or west a point is from another, varies depending on the latitude. This is explained in more detail in the program distance_gps.py.

The program "walks around" the polygon, connecting the first coordinate in the list sequentially with pairs of coordinates around the edges of the polygon to form small triangles. The sum of the areas of these triangles is the area of the whole figure defined by the list of coordinates. Here we'll use the distance and direction angle between any two coordinates to calculate the area of smaller triangular areas in the polygon.

The triangles.py program elsewhere in this book demonstrates how to find all the parts of a triangle, including its area, given any combination of three of its sides and angles. The side-angle-side function is borrowed from that program to find the areas of small triangles.

The really cool thing is that even if the polygon shape defined by the coordinates has concavities, the program automatically adds and subtracts the areas correctly. This works because the angle between the selected pairs of points and the first point is usually positive during the "walk around". But with a concavity, one or more of the angles is negative, and the area of the small triangle is then calculated as a negative. It all works out, where the overlapping areas add and subtract correctly and automatically to get an accurate total area.

First, let's look at a fairly simple example.

The Pentagon building in Arlington, Virginia has five sides, and five GPS coordinates on its corners. Google Maps lets us find the latitude and longitude of any point on the map (right-click on a point and select "What's here?" from the popup menu.) Here are the corner coordinates I found, in standard latitude, longitude notation:

38.868868, -77.055655

38.870619, -77.053325

38.872875, -77.054717

38.872532, -77.057948

38.870039, -77.058504

The program first finds the area of triangle 0,1,2 where point 0 is the first coordinate in the list:

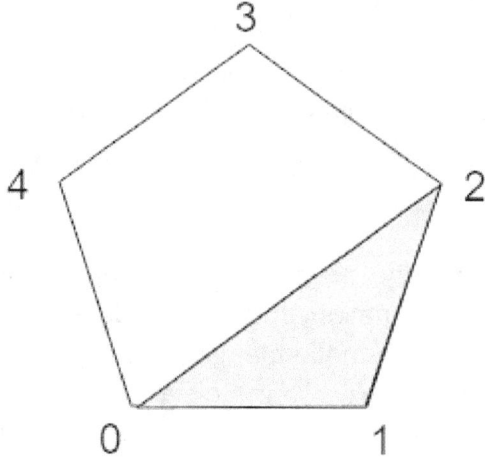

The pentagon "walk around" next finds the area of triangle 0,2,3, as shown here:

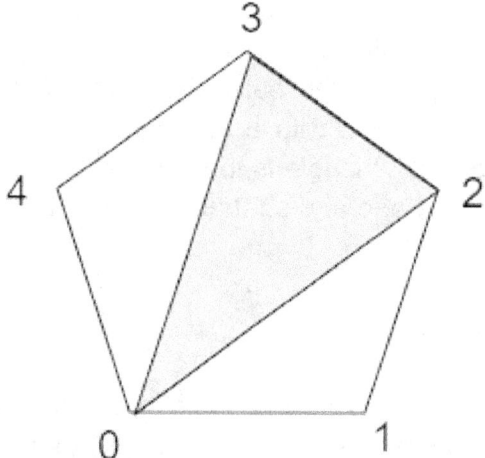

Finally, the area of triangle 0,3,4 is found and added to the other areas to find the total area of the Pentagon's pentagon:

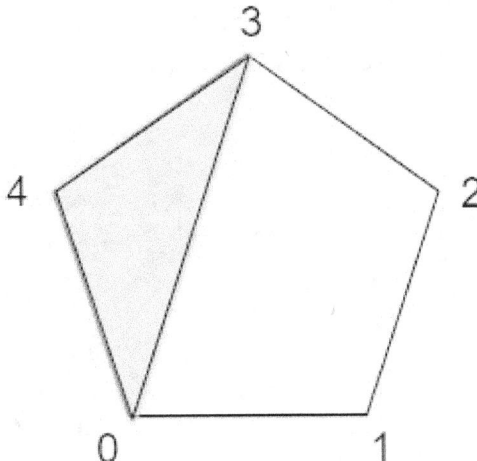

The program lets you either enter the coordinates on the fly, at runtime, or you can set them up by editing the pts list in the function load_gps(). I prefer to do it this way, especially with longer lists of coordinates, because it's easier to check them over, make changes, and rerun the program. As shown in the program listing, I've edited the Pentagon coordinates into the program.

Run the program and an area of about 0.135 square kilometers is the result. A quick conversion shows this to be about 33 ⅓ acres. I checked on the Internet and found several estimates of the Pentagon's size, all in fairly close agreement to this value.

```
>>> from area_gps import *
1. ask_gps
2. load_gps
? 2
km^2:   0.1351176142591852
>>>
```

The second example calculates the surface area, very roughly, of Turquoise Lake, near Leadville, Colorado. Here's a quick sketch (courtesy of Google Maps) of the area we'll find, as defined by four points I selected on the map:

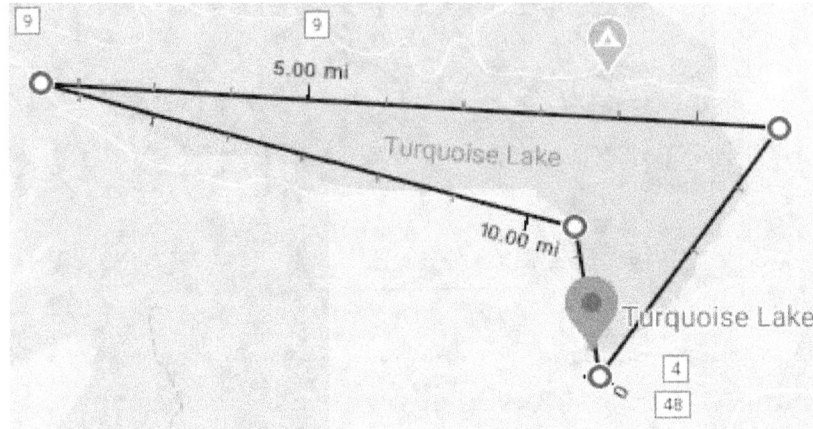

The four map coordinates, starting at the bottom point and working around counter-clockwise, are:

39.249968, -106.370986

39.273513, -106.348860

39.277695, -106.438465

39.264220, -106.373614

I chose this lake, and this shape, on purpose, because there's a concavity at the bottom left, at the last coordinate, labeled 3:

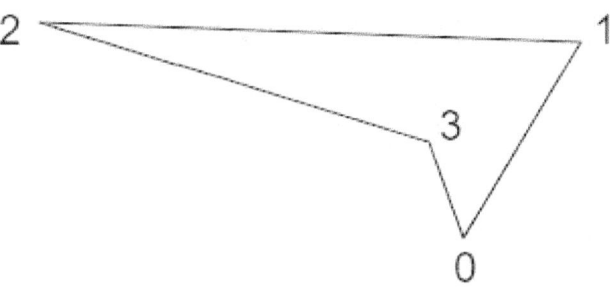

The first triangle area is found at 0,1,2 as shown here:

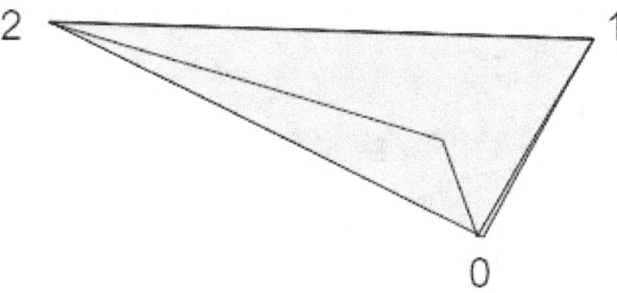

Notice that this triangle is too big, covering more area than the overall lake outline. That's okay though, as the next triangle, at 0,2,3 is "backwards", in that the order of its points is clockwise instead of counter-clockwise, resulting in a negative area.

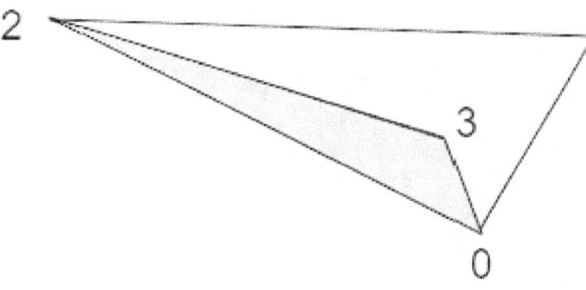

No matter how complicated the list of coordinates gets, as long as they are in the correct "walk around" order for the entire polygon, all the areas total up correctly, both positive and negative, and no matter how they overlap.

In this case, I entered the coordinates manually, at run time:

```
>>> from area_gps import *
1. ask_gps
2. load_gps
? 1
Coordinate  1
Lat: 39.249968
Lon: -106.370986
Coordinate  2
Lat:
```

```
Lat: 39.273513
Lon: -106.348860
Coordinate  3
Lat: 39.277695
Lon: -106.438465
Coordinate  4
Lat: 39.264220
Lon: -106.373614
Coordinate  5
Lat:
km^2:   6.288697481814668
>>>
```

6.289 square kilometers is about 1,554 acres. A quick check on the Internet shows the area of Turquoise Lake to be 1,780 acres. Considering how crude our outline of the lake was, with just four points to define it, our calculation is pretty good!

This program works well for land areas that aren't too large. The Earth is not flat, so the curve of the Earth's surface does affect calculated areas if they are very large, say hundreds of kilometers on edge.

```python
# area_gps.py
from math import *

def area_gps(pts):
    area=0
    if len(pts)>2:
        n=2
        while n<len(pts):
            x0,y0=pts[0]
            x1,y1=pts[n-1]
            x2,y2=pts[n]
            b1,a=nav(x0,y0,x1,y1)
            b2,b=nav(x0,y0,x2,y2)
            b1=b1 if b1>0 else b1+360
            b2=b2 if b2>0 else b2+360
            C=b1-b2
            area+=area_sas(b,C,a)
            n+=1
    return area

def ask_gps():
    pts=[]
    while True:
        try:
            print("Coordinate ",len(pts)+1)
            la=float(input("Lat: "))
            lo=float(input("Lon: "))
            pts.append([la,lo])
        except:
            break
    return pts
```

```
def load_gps():
  pts=[]
  pts.append([38.868868, -77.055655]) #0
  pts.append([38.870619, -77.053325]) #1
  pts.append([38.872875, -77.054717]) #2
  pts.append([38.872532, -77.057948]) #3
  pts.append([38.870039, -77.058504]) #4
  return pts

def nav(la1,lo1,la2,lo2):
  la1=radians(la1)
  lo1=radians(lo1)
  la2=radians(la2)
  lo2=radians(lo2)
  r=6371
  t1=sin(la1)*sin(la2)
  t2=cos(la1)*cos(la2)*cos(lo2-lo1)
  km=acos(t1+t2)*r
  y=sin(lo2-lo1)*cos(la2)
  t1=cos(la1)*sin(la2)
  t2=sin(la1)*cos(la2)*cos(lo2-lo1)
  x=t1-t2
  b=degrees(atan2(y,x))
  return [b,km]

def area_sas(a,C,b):
  return a*b*sin(radians(C))/2

print("1. ask_gps")
print("2. load_gps")
n=int(input("? "))
if n==1:
  pts=ask_gps()
else:
  pts=load_gps()
area=area_gps(pts)
print("km^2: ",area)
```

distance_gps.py

Distance between two points in a plane is found using the Pythagorean Theorem, but distances on the surface of a sphere, such as the Earth, is more complicated. This program accurately calculates the distance between any two locations given their latitude and longitude coordinates, also referred to as GPS coordinates.

The algorithm uses several trigonometric functions, so the math module is imported at the top of the listing. The sin() and cos() functions in Python assume all angles are in radians, so the radians() function in the math module is used to convert latitude and longitude from standard degrees to radians. (Yes, there is a degrees() function as well, but it's not used in this program.)

The distance() function is at the heart of this program. Inputs are latitude and longitude for two points on the Earth, and output is the kilometers between the two points. The constant 6371 is the radius of the Earth in kilometers.

For example, the Gateway Arch in St. Louis is visible on Google Maps, and we can carefully zoom in and click to find the coordinates at back corners of the Arch where the metal meets the concrete. Those are the pair of coordinates in the program listing. Another coordinate is at the Golden Gate Bridge in San Francisco, so we can measure a greater distance as well.

The St. Louis Arch is 630 feet tall and 630 feet wide. This program calculates the width as 629.9 feet, which is a very good result! The air (straight-line) distance between San Francisco and St. Louis is listed as 1745 km, and this program finds the distance between the Arch and the Bridge as 1744.7 miles, which is also an amazingly similar result:

```
>>> from distance_gps import >
Arch Meters:   192.00541384309&
Arch Feet:   629.93904195299
Arch-Bridge km:   2807.8905900:
Arch-Bridge miles:   1744.7417&
>>> |
```

```python
# distance_gps.py
from math import *

def distance(la1,lo1,la2,lo2):
  la1=radians(la1)
  lo1=radians(lo1)
  la2=radians(la2)
  lo2=radians(lo2)
  r=6371
  t1=sin(la1)*sin(la2)
  t2=cos(la1)*cos(la2)*cos(lo2-lo1)
  km=acos(t1+t2)*r
  return km
```

```
#Arch width
la1=38.625412
lo1=-90.184555
la2=38.623767
lo2=-90.185227
km=distance(la1,lo1,la2,lo2)
print("Arch Meters: ",km*1000)
print("Arch Feet: ",km*3280.84)

#Arch to Golden Gate Bridge
la2=37.820142
lo2=-122.478709
km=distance(la1,lo1,la2,lo2)
print("Arch-Bridge km: ",km)
print("Arch-Bridge miles: ",km*.621371)
```

great_circle.py

This program calculates the distance and bearing between any two points on the surface of the Earth.

It's easy to find the location of a point on Earth using Google Maps. Zoom in to the location, right-click on the point, and select "What's Here?" from the popup menu. That's a good way to get the latitude and longitude numbers required as input for this program.

The great circle route formula used here is accurate for short distances, such as measuring a short stretch of sidewalk in front of a school, and it's also accurate for much longer distances where the spherical shape of the Earth becomes very important.

The location, or GPS coordinates taken from Google Maps, of Dulce, NM and Taos, NM are hard coded into the program to test it out. Feel free to change these numbers, or to change the program to have it prompt for inputs. The core functionality is in the nav() function, so call it any way that you wish.

As shown, the distance from Dulce to Taos is very close to 140 km, and the direction to head is 114.3 degrees, or just a little south of due east.

```
>>> from great_circle import *
km:    139.9862544058342
Bearing:   114.2894596804861
>>>
```

```python
# great_circle.py
from math import *

def nav(la1,lo1,la2,lo2):
    la1=radians(la1)
    lo1=radians(lo1)
    la2=radians(la2)
    lo2=radians(lo2)
    r=6371
    t1=sin(la1)*sin(la2)
    t2=cos(la1)*cos(la2)*cos(lo2-lo1)
    km=acos(t1+t2)*r
    t1=cos(la1)*sin(la2)
    t2=sin(la1)*cos(la2)*cos(lo2-lo1)
    x=t1-t2
    y=sin(lo2-lo1)*cos(la2)
    b=degrees(atan2(y,x))
    return [b,km]

# Dulce, NM
la1=36.9336
lo1=-106.9989

# Taos, NM
la2=36.4072
lo2=-105.5731

# Distance and bearing
b,km=nav(la1,lo1,la2,lo2)
print("km: ",km)
print("Bearing: ",b)
```

midpoint.py

This program finds the latitude and longitude at a point halfway between two other locations on the Earth. Call up your friend a state or two away and have them meet you at the exact midpoint, just for fun.

This program is also great for checking if the Earth is flat or round. Seriously. Consider that the Sun's elevation angle can be easily measured with a simple meter stick on a sunny day. I won't go into all the details here, but note that the elevation angle of the Sun as measured from three equidistant points on the Earth, will provide all the information you need. If the Earth is flat, the elevation angles will behave one way, and if the Earth is round the angles will behave another way. *(Spoiler Alert: The Earth is round.)*

Let's find the latitude and longitude of the point halfway between the Golden Gate Bridge in San Francisco, and the Gateway Arch in St. Louis.

Here's the location of one corner of the arch, as we used in the distance_gps.py program:

la1=38.625412
lo1=-90.184555

And here's the Golden Gate Bridge coordinate from the same program:

la2=37.820142
lo2=-122.478709

Let's plug those coordinates into the program, find the midpoint on the Earth, and then look up that point on Google Maps to see what's there:

```
>>> from midpoint import *
Lat1: 38.625412
Lon1: -90.184555
Lat2: 37.820142
Lon2: -122.478709
Lat midpoint:   39.34866732560:
Lon midpoint:   -106.423442472!
>>>
```

The midpoint is in a very picturesque place along the West Tennessee Creek, just a little northwest of Leadville, Colorado. That would be a fun place to meet your friend!

```
# midpoint
from math import *

def mid(la1,lo1,la2,lo2):
  la1=radians(la1)
  lo1=radians(lo1)
  la2=radians(la2)
  lo2=radians(lo2)
  x=cos(la1)*cos(lo1)
  y=cos(la1)*sin(lo1)
  z=sin(la1)
  x+=cos(la2)*cos(lo2)
  y+=cos(la2)*sin(lo2)
  z+=sin(la2)
  la=degrees(atan2(z,(x*x+y*y)**.5))
  lo=degrees(atan2(y,x))
  return [la,lo]

lat1=float(input("Lat1: "))
lon1=float(input("Lon1: "))
lat2=float(input("Lat2: "))
lon2=float(input("Lon2: "))
latm,lonm=mid(lat1,lon1,lat2,lon2)
print("Lat midpoint: ",latm)
print("Lon midpoint: ",lonm)
```

6.

Money and Finances

This chapter presents several programs to calculate interest, savings, loans and other details having to do with the flow of money.

The next time you're ready to buy a car, or house, or game console, you can see how much the loan will cost you in interest, or better yet, how long it will take to save up to pay cash.

future_val.py

Saving up for something you want to purchase in the future is a great way to make your money go further. The money accumulates at some interest rate, instead of having to pay out interest on a loan, so you basically save in two ways. This program lets you experiment to see just how much you'll save, and to help you stay on target as you invest in yourself.

You are prompted for the amount of money you can provide each month, the annual interest rate that the money will accumulate more value, and the number of years to tally the total. The future value is output. In the example shown, $50 is put away each month, at an accumulating annual interest rate of 7%, and the future value after 3 years, totalling $1996.51 is the output.

```
>>> from future_val import *
Monthly deposit: 50
Interest rate: 7
Years: 3
Future value: $1996.51
>>>
```

```python
# future_val.py
dp=float(input("Monthly deposit: "))
ir=float(input("Interest rate: "))
yr=float(input("Years: "))
ir/=1200
mo=yr*12
fv=dp*((ir+1)**mo-1)/ir
print("Future value: ${:,.2f}".format(fv))
```

interest.py

This program calculates the interest rate being charged for a loan when the principal, monthly payment amount, and the number of months to make the payments are known. The calculated annual interest rate is output.

The example shows an annual percentage rate of 10.49% is being charged for a loan of $10,000 with monthly payments of $325 over a 3 year period, or 36 months.

```
>>> from interest import *
Principal: 10000
Monthly payments: 325
Months: 36
APR: 10.49%
>>>
```

```
# interest.py
p=float(input("Principal: "))
pmt=float(input("Monthly payments: "))
n=float(input("Months: "))
r=1
t=0
while t!=r:
    t=r
    r=pmt*((1+r)**n-1)/p/(1+r)**n
i=round(r*1200,2)
print("APR: {}%".format(i))
```

loan.py

This program calculates monthly payments for a loan given the amount, or principal of the loan, the annual percentage rate, and the number of monthly payments to be made.

The example shows a loan of $5000 at 9% interest rate will require 24 monthly payments of $228.42.

```
>>> from loan import *
Principal: 5000
Annual Interest: 9
Months: 24
Monthly payments: $228.42
>>>
```

```python
# loan.py
p=float(input("Principal: "))
r=float(input("Annual Interest: "))/1200
n=float(input("Months: "))
pmt=p*(r*(1+r)**n)/((1+r)**n-1)
s="Monthly payments: ${}"
print(s.format(round(pmt,2)))
```

principal.py

Given the monthly payment amount for a loan, the annual percentage rate for the loan, and the number of months to pay the loan off, this program calculates the original principal of the loan.

For example, given payments of $228.42 monthly for 24 months at 9% interest, the original loan amount was $4999.92. The actual amount of the loan was probably $5000, because slight roundoff errors can accumulate to a few cents pretty easily, as in this case.

```
>>> from principal import *
Monthly payments: 228.42
Annual Interest: 9
Months: 24
Principal: $4999.92
>>>
```

```
# principal.py
pmt=float(input("Monthly payments: "))
r=float(input("Annual Interest: "))/1200
n=float(input("Months: "))
p=pmt/(r*(1+r)**n)*((1+r)**n-1)
s="Principal: ${:.2f}"
print(s.format(p))
```

reg_deposits.py

This program helps you save for a goal by calculating how much money to put away in an interest bearing account, and for how long, in order to reach your goal.

For example, perhaps you want to get a new gaming laptop that costs $1000, and you want it one year from today. As shown, you should start putting away $80.69 each month in an account that earns 7% interest.

```
>>> from reg_deposits import *
Dollars goal: 1000
Interest rate: 7
Months: 12
Monthly deposits: $80.69
>>>
```

```python
# reg_deposits
fv=float(input("Dollars goal: "))
ir=float(input("Interest rate: "))
mo=float(input("Months: "))
ir/=1200
dp=fv/((ir+1)**mo-1)*ir
s="Monthly deposits: ${:.2f}"
print(s.format(dp))
```

7.

Plane Geometry

At the heart of most digital gaming systems are many calculations critical for simulating the real world. This chapter presents common two-dimensional calculations and coordinate transformations used for many purposes, including creating all types of graphics and game animations.

arcs.py

GIven any two of the four parameters describing part of a circle, this program calculates the two unknown parts. The parts are arc length, chord length, the central angle and the radius for the circle that defines the arc.

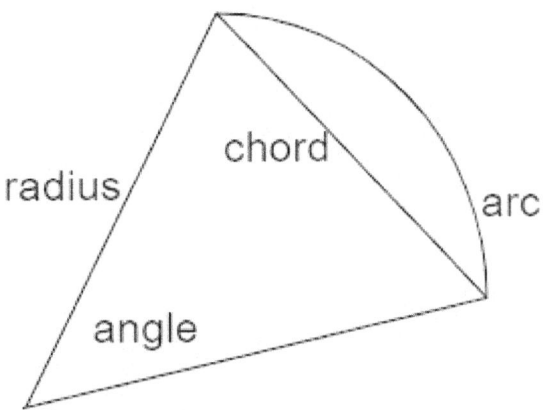

For example, suppose a railroad track is to be designed to make a 45 degree turn, where the straight-line (chord) distance between the endpoints of the turn is 2,021 meters. How long is the track? As shown in the example, the track (arc length), is about 2,074 meters.

```
Input two known values

Angle (deg): 45
Radius:
Chord length: 2021
Arc length:

Angle:   45.0
Radius:   2640.563752015157
Chord:   2021.0
Arc:    2073.893921166579
>>>
```

```python
from math import *

def arcs(a,r,c,s):
  if a:
    if r:
      s=r*a
    elif c:
      r=c/2/sin(a/2)
    else:
      r=s/a
  elif r:
    if c:
      a=2*asin(c/r/2)
    else:
      a=s/r
  else:
    a=.1
    t=0
    while a!=t:
      t=a
      a=2*s*sin(a/2)/c
    r=s/a
  c=2*r*sin(a/2)
  s=r*a
  return [a,r,c,s]
```

```python
print("\n\nInput two known values\n")
a=input("Angle (deg): ")
a=float(a) if a else 0
a=radians(a)
r=input("Radius: ")
r=float(r) if r else 0
c=input("Chord length: ")
c=float(c) if c else 0
s=input("Arc length: ")
s=float(s) if s else 0
a,r,c,s=arcs(a,r,c,s)
a=degrees(a)
print("\nAngle: ",a)
print("Radius: ",r)
print("Chord: ",c)
print("Arc: ",s)
```

area_3p.py

Three x,y points in a plane define a triangle. This program calculates the area of a triangle given any three points.

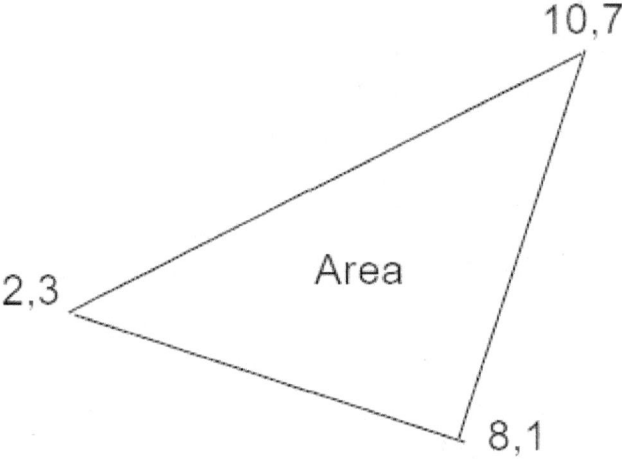

In the example shown, after entering the three coordinates, the area of the triangle is calculated as 20 square units.

```
>>> from area_3p import *
x1: 2
y1: 3
x2: 8
y2: 1
x3: 10
y3: 7
Area:   20.0
>>>
```

```python
# area_3p.py
def area_3p(p1,p2,p3):
  x1,y1=p1
  x2,y2=p2
  x3,y3=p3
  a=x1*y2+x2*y3+x3*y1
  b=x1*y3+x2*y1+x3*y2
  return abs((a-b)/2)

x=float(input("x1: "))
y=float(input("y1: "))
p1=[x,y]
x=float(input("x2: "))
y=float(input("y2: "))
p2=[x,y]
x=float(input("x3: "))
y=float(input("y3: "))
p3=[x,y]
print("Area: ",area_3p(p1,p2,p3))
```

area_3s.py

Heron's formula lets us find the area of a triangle if the lengths of its three sides are known, without having to calculate angles or other distances first. Here's the formula, given sides with lengths a, b, and c:

$$s = \frac{a+b+c}{2}$$

$$Area = \sqrt{s(s-a)(s-b)(s-c)}$$

For example, what is the area of a triangle that has sides of 7, 11, and 17 cm? Input these three values into the program and the answer is calculated to be approximately 24.44 square cm.

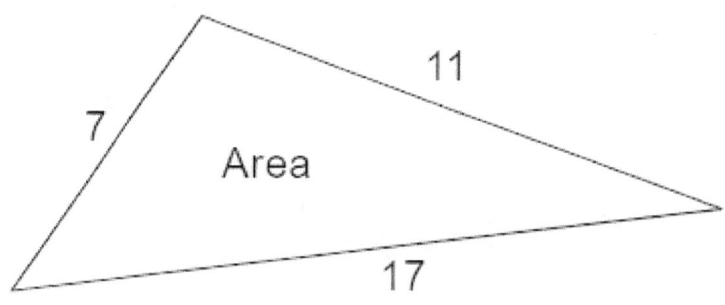

```
>>> from area_3s import *
Side a: 7
Side b: 11
Side c: 17
Area:  24.43742007659565
>>>
```

```python
# area_3s.py
def area_3s(a,b,c):
    s=(a+b+c)/2
    return (s*(s-a)*(s-b)*(s-c))**.5

a=float(input("Side a: "))
b=float(input("Side b: "))
c=float(input("Side c: "))
print("Area: ",area_3s(a,b,c))
```

area_np.py

This program computes the area of a polygon of any shape. The X,Y coordinates of each vertex are input either at runtime, or by editing a list of points directly in the code. When the polygon has many points around its perimeter it's usually easier to edit the points directly in the code.

Enter the points by "walking around" the polygon in either direction. The program listing shows an example polygon with six vertices, as shown here:

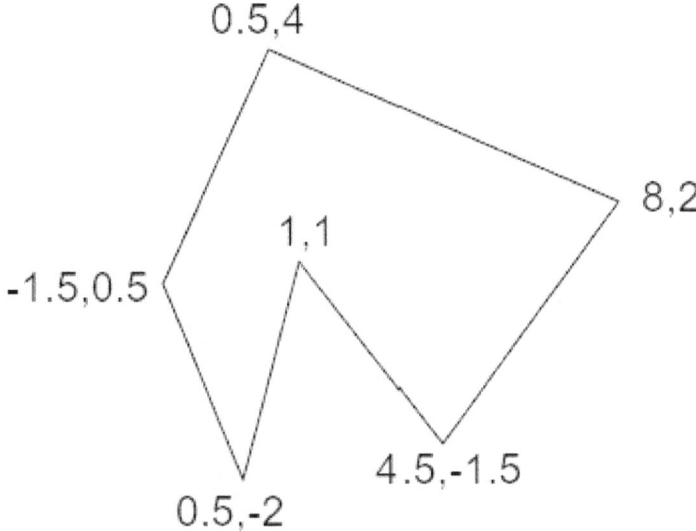

These points are edited directly in the program listing, so choose 2 to call load_pts() when the program starts. The area is then quickly calculated as 28.75.

```
>>> from area_np import *
1. ask_pts
2. load_pts
? 2
Area:   28.75
>>>
```

```python
# area_np
from math import *

def load_pts():
    pts=[]
    pts.append([4.5,-1.5])
    pts.append([8,2])
    pts.append([.5,4])
    pts.append([-1.5,.5])
    pts.append([.5,-2])
    pts.append([1,1])
    return pts

def area_pts(pts):
    area=0
    pts.append(pts[0])
    for i in range(len(pts)-1):
        a=pts[i][0]+pts[i+1][0]
        b=pts[i][1]-pts[i+1][1]
        area+=a*b
    return abs(area/2)
```

```
def ask_pts():
  pts=[]
  while True:
    try:
      print("Coordinate ",len(pts)+1)
      x=float(input("x: "))
      y=float(input("y: "))
      pts.append([x,y])
    except:
      break
  return pts

print("1. ask_pts")
print("2. load_pts")
n=int(input("? "))
if n==1:
  pts=ask_pts()
else:
  pts=load_pts()
area=area_pts(pts)
print("Area: ",area)
```

circle.py

This program finds the center and radius of a circle that just touches three points in the x,y plane. Another way to put this is the program finds a point that is equidistant from three given points. Of course this won't work if the three points are in a straight line. The program detects this condition and prints "Not a circle" if this is the case.

For example, find a circle that passes through the points (3,12), (10,13), and (7,4):

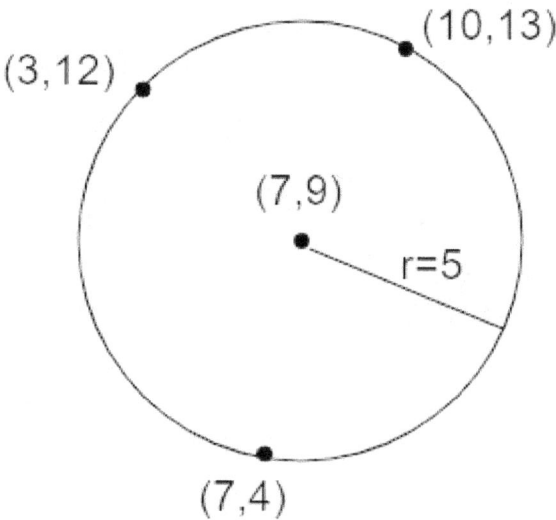

Enter the three points and the program calculates the circle's center at the point (7,9), and a radius of 5 units.

```
>>> from circle import *
x1: 3
y1: 12
x2: 10
y2: 13
x3: 7
y3: 4
xc:  7.0
yc:  9.0
r:  5.0
>>> 
```

```python
# circle.py
x1=float(input("x1: "))
y1=float(input("y1: "))
x2=float(input("x2: "))
y2=float(input("y2: "))
x3=float(input("x3: "))
y3=float(input("y3: "))
A=(x1*(y2-y3)-
   y1*(x2-x3)+
   x2*y3-x3*y2)
B=((x1*x1+y1*y1)*
   (y3-y2)+
   (x2*x2+y2*y2)*
   (y1-y3)+
   (x3*x3+y3*y3)*
   (y2-y1))
C=((x1*x1+y1*y1)*
   (x2-x3)+
   (x2*x2+y2*y2)*
   (x3-x1)+
   (x3*x3+y3*y3)*
   (x1-x2))
```

```python
if A==0:
    print("Not a circle")
else:
    xc=-B/A/2
    yc=-C/A/2
    r=(((xc-x1)**2+
    (yc-y1)**2)**.5)
    print("xc: ",xc)
    print("yc: ",yc)
    print("r: ",r)
```

divide_line.py

This program presents two functions that split a line in the x,y plane into parts. Often, just the midpoint of a line segment is desired, and that is what the midpoint() function returns. To find equidistant points along a line segment that split the segment into n equal parts, call the divide_line() function.

The example code splits a line segment from point (3,2) to point (9,5) into three equal parts, and it finds the midpoint too.

```
>>> from divide_line import *
x1: 3
y1: 2
x2: 9
y2: 5
Segs: 3
```

As soon as the number of segments is input, the results are calculated and displayed. If you split the line into a lot of pieces, you can scroll the display to see all the results.

```
y1: 2
x2: 9
y2: 5
Segs: 3
[3.0, 2.0]
[5.0, 3.0]
[7.0, 4.0]
[9.0, 5.0]

xm:   6.0
ym:   3.5
>>>
```

```python
# divide_line.py
def midpoint(x1,y1,x2,y2):
  p1=[x1,y1]
  p2=[x2,y2]
  mp=divide_line(p1,p2,2)
  return mp[1]

def divide_line(p1,p2,n):
  pts=[]
  for i in range(n+1):
    x=p1[0]+(p2[0]-p1[0])*i/n
    y=p1[1]+(p2[1]-p1[1])*i/n
    pts.append([x,y])
  return pts

x1=float(input("x1: "))
y1=float(input("y1: "))
x2=float(input("x2: "))
y2=float(input("y2: "))
segs=int(input("Segs: "))
pts=divide_line([x1,y1],[x2,y2],segs)
for pt in pts:
  print(pt)
xm,ym=midpoint(x1,y1,x2,y2)
print("")
print("xm: ",xm)
print("ym: ",ym)
```

lines.py

This program calculates several features of a line in a plane, given either two points along the line, or one point and the line's slope. For example, given the point 4,3 and the slope -0.5, what does this tell us about a line with these parameters?

```
What is known?
1. Two points
2. Point and slope
? 2
Point x? 4
Point y? 3
Slope m? -.5
m =    -0.5
xi =    10.0
yi =    5.0
y=-0.5*x+5.0
>>>
```

The slope (m) is -0.5, the x intercept (xi) is 10.0, and the y intercept (yi) is 5.0. Here's a sketch of the line in question, and the equation of the line, as shown in the last line of the program's output:

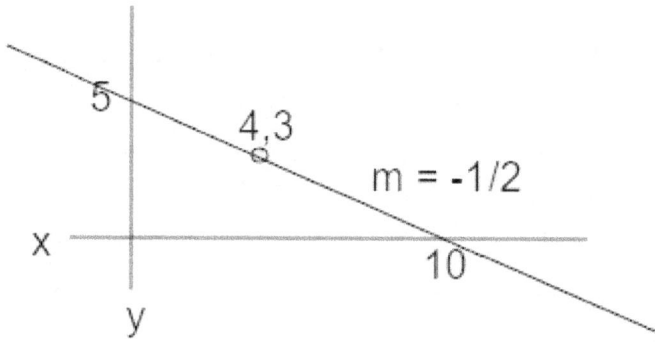

$$y = -0.5x + 5.0$$

```python
# lines.py
print("What is known?")
print("1. Two points")
print("2. Point and slope")
n = int(input("? "))
if n==1:
  x1 = float(input("Point 1, x? "))
  y1 = float(input("Point 1, y? "))
  x2 = float(input("Point 2, x? "))
  y2 = float(input("Point 2, y? "))
  m = (y2 - y1) / (x2 - x1)
elif n==2:
  x1 = float(input("Point x? "))
  y1 = float(input("Point y? "))
  m = float(input("Slope m? "))
else:
  print("Please try again")
yi = y1-m*x1
xi = x1-y1/m
print("m = ", m)
print("xi = ", xi)
print("yi = ", yi)
f="y={}*x+{}"
if yi<0: f=f.replace("+","")
print(f.format(m,yi))
```

rotate.py

Computer graphics games require a lot of high speed math to keep the action realistic and smooth. One of the core algorithms is the ability to rotate a point in the x,y plane around the origin by some angle. This is a huge simplification of the requirements of game programming, but hey, it's a start!

This program lets you input an x,y coordinate, and a rotation amount in degrees. The rotate() function takes this coordinate, plus the angle converted to radians, and returns the new coordinate after the rotation.

For example, the point (2,3) will end up near (1.035,3.454) after a rotation of 17 degrees around the origin.

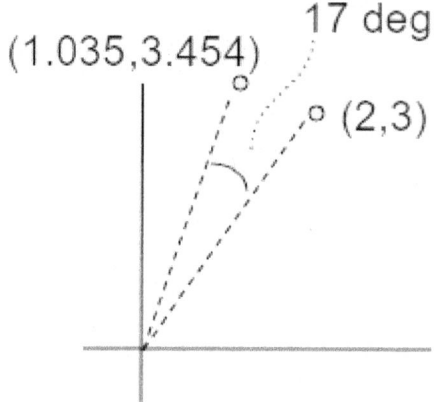

```
>>> from rotate import *
x: 2
y: 3
deg: 17
x:    1.035494397757861
y:    3.45365767733458
>>>
```

Study this program to learn more about how to input floating point numbers, using trigonometric functions, and how to return two values from a function by wrapping them in a list and unpacking them into two variables upon the return.

```
# rotate.py
from math import *

def rotate(x,y,a):
   xr=x*cos(a)-y*sin(a)
   yr=x*sin(a)+y*cos(a)
   return [xr,yr]

x=float(input("x: "))
y=float(input("y: "))
a=float(input("deg: "))
a=radians(a)
x,y=rotate(x,y,a)
print("x: ",x)
print("y: ",y)
```

triangles.py

This program solves for all sides, angles, and the area of a triangle given any combination of three of its sides or angles.

There are five combinations of sides and angles possible. If s represents a side, and a represents an angle, then the combinations that can occur as you walk around the triangle's edges and angles sequentially are: sss, sas, ssa, asa, and aas. This program asks which condition is known, then prompts for those three parts and calculates all the rest, plus the area.

The output parts are labeled s1, s2, and s3 for the sides, and a1, a2, a3 for the angles opposite those sides. Area is the last item output.

For example, what are the angles and area for a triangle with sides 4, 5 and 6?

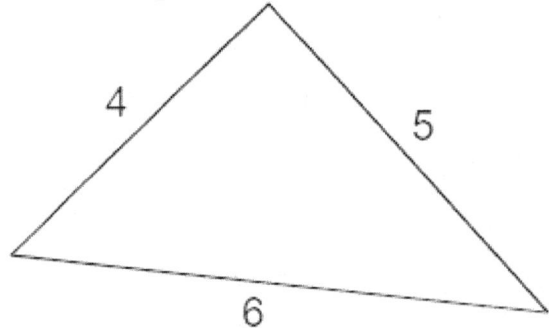

```
>>> from triangles import *
1. sss
2. sas
3. ssa
4. asa
5. aas
? 1
s: 4
s: 5
s: 6
```

Enter 1 for sss at the first prompt, then enter the lengths of the sides. Once all three parts are entered the results are calculated and displayed:

```
? 1
s: 4
s: 5
s: 6
s1:  4.0
s2:  5.0
s3:  6.0
a1:  41.40962210927086
a2:  55.77113367218743
a3:  82.81924421854171
Area:  9.921567416492215
>>>
```

Opposite the side with length 4 is an angle of about 41.4 degrees, and so on. The triangle's area is a little over 9.92 square units.

```python
# triangles.py
from math import *

def sss(a,b,c):
  A=degrees(acos((b*b+c*c-a*a)/b/c/2))
  B=degrees(acos((a*a+c*c-b*b)/a/c/2))
  C=180-A-B
  return [a,b,c,A,B,C]

def sas(a,C,b):
  c=(a*a+b*b-2*a*b*cos(radians(C)))**.5
  A=degrees(acos((b*b+c*c-a*a)/(2*b*c)))
  B=180-A-C
  return [a,b,c,A,B,C]

def ssa(b,c,B):
  C=degrees(asin(c*sin(radians(B))/b))
  A=180-B-C
  a=b*sin(radians(A))/sin(radians(B))
  return [a,b,c,A,B,C]

def asa(A,c,B):
  C=180-A-B
  a=c*sin(radians(A))/sin(radians(C))
  b=c*sin(radians(B))/sin(radians(C))
  return [a,b,c,A,B,C]

def aas(A,C,a):
  B=180-A-C
  b=a*sin(radians(B))/sin(radians(A))
  c=a*sin(radians(C))/sin(radians(A))
  return [a,b,c,A,B,C]
```

```python
# Heron's formula
def area(a,b,c):
  p=(a+b+c)/2
  return (p*(p-a)*(p-b)*(p-c))**.5

print("1. sss")
print("2. sas")
print("3. ssa")
print("4. asa")
print("5. aas")
n=int(input("? "))
if n<4:
  a=input("s: ")
  a=float(a) if a else 0
else:
  A=input("Ang A: ")
  A=float(A) if A else 0
if n==1 or n==3 or n==4:
  b=input("s: ")
  b=float(b) if b else 0
else:
  B=input("Ang B: ")
  B=float(B) if B else 0
if n<3 or n==5:
  c=input("s: ")
  c=float(c) if c else 0
else:
  C=input("Ang C: ")
  C=float(C) if C else 0
if n==1:
  t=sss(a,b,c)
if n==2:
  t=sas(a,B,c)
if n==3:
  t=ssa(a,b,C)
if n==4:
  t=asa(A,b,C)
```

```
if n==5:
  t=aas(A,B,c)
ar=area(t[0],t[1],t[2])
print("s1: ",t[0])
print("s2: ",t[1])
print("s3: ",t[2])
print("a1: ",t[3])
print("a2: ",t[4])
print("a3: ",t[5])
print("Area: ",ar)
```

triangles_3p.py

This program calculates the sides, angles, and area of a triangle given three points in the x,y plane.

For example, what are sides, angles, and area of a triangle defined by the points (2,4), (10,4), and (2,10)?

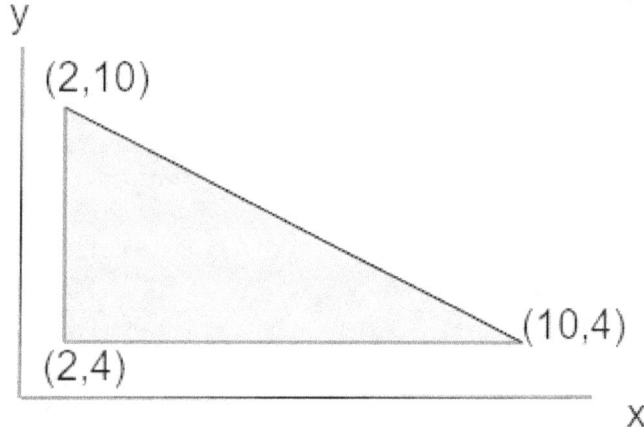

Enter the coordinates as prompted.

```
>>> from triangles_3p import ›
x1: 2
y1: 4
x2: 10
y2: 4
x3: 2
y3: 10
```

Once the third x,y coordinate is entered the results are calculated and displayed.

```
x2: 10
y2: 4
x3: 2
y3: 10
s(1-2):   8.0
s(1-3):   6.0
s(2-3):   10.0
a(1):   90.0
a(2):   36.86989764584402
a(3):   53.13010235415599
area:   24.0
>>>
```

s(1-2) indicates the side connecting the 1st and 2nd points entered. a(1) indicates the angle at the first point entered.

```
# triangles_3p.py
from math import *

x1=float(input("x1: "))
y1=float(input("y1: "))
x2=float(input("x2: "))
y2=float(input("y2: "))
x3=float(input("x3: "))
y3=float(input("y3: "))
a=((y2-y1)**2+(x2-x1)**2)**.5
b=((y3-y1)**2+(x3-x1)**2)**.5
c=((y3-y2)**2+(x3-x2)**2)**.5
```

```
A=degrees(acos((b*b+c*c-a*a)/b/c/2))
B=degrees(acos((a*a+c*c-b*b)/a/c/2))
C=180-A-B
area=a*b*sin(radians(C))/2
print("s(1-2): ",a)
print("s(1-3): ",b)
print("s(2-3): ",c)
print("a(1): ",C)
print("a(2): ",B)
print("a(3): ",A)
print("area: ",area)
```

two_points.py

Two points determine a line, and this program tells you a little about that line. You enter two x,y coordinates, and out pops the slope of the connecting line, and the distance between the two points.

For example, given the points (2,3) and (6,5) in the x,y plane, what is the distance between them, and what is the slope of the connecting line?

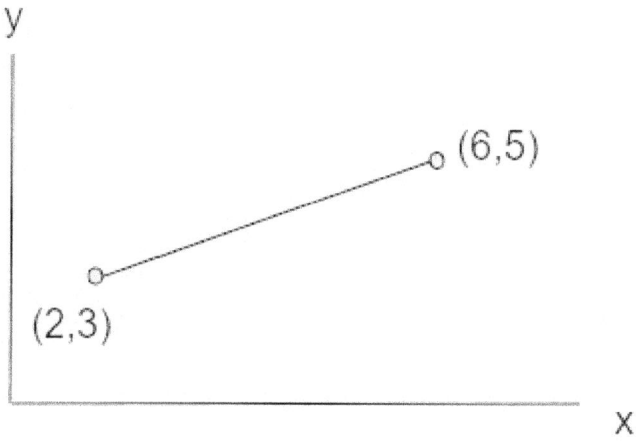

Run the program and enter the points to get the answers.

```
>>> from two_points import *
x1: 2
y1: 3
x2: 6
y2: 5
dist:   4.47213595499958
slope:  0.5
>>>
```

The points are about 4.47 units apart, and the slope between them is 0.5, or one-half.

```python
# two_points.py
x1=float(input("x1: "))
y1=float(input("y1: "))
x2=float(input("x2: "))
y2=float(input("y2: "))
dx=x2-x1
dy=y2-y1
dist=(dx**2+dy**2)**.5
slope=dy/dx if dx else 1e999
print("dist: ",dist)
print("slope: ",slope)
```

8.

Space Geometry

The previous chapter presented several programs to work with lines, arcs, triangles, and other constructs in a two-dimensional plane. This chapter extends those concepts into three dimensions.

3D games require rotations around each of the three axes in order to move characters and objects around in space. There are powerful ways to accomplish this using matrices, but even the matrix math depends on the ability to mathematically rotate around each axis. You'll find functions to do these rotations in this chapter.

In two dimensions, a set of three points determines a triangle. This is true with sets of three space points as well. Also, in three dimensions a set of four space points determines a tetrahedron-like volume. You'll find programs to do these calculations in this chapter.

coord_3d.py

There are three common coordinate systems used to designate a point's coordinates in space. Cartesian coordinates use x,y,z values, similar to x,y in a plane but extended into space with a z direction. Cylindrical coordinates use a radius and angle in the x,y plane to determine a point directly "below" the point, and a z value for the distance to it from the x,y plane. Spherical coordinates use a radial distance from the origin, and two angles to determine the angle in the x,y plane and the angle away from the z axis.

In this program the variables x,y,z refer to distances along their respective axes. ra and th (short for theta) are the radius and angle for cylindrical coordinates, and rh, th, ph (short for rho, theta, phi) are used for spherical coordinates.

Six functions are provided, allowing conversions from any of the three coordinate systems to any of the others. Pass the three known coordinate values and the coordinate values will be returned in a list. Notice in the example source code that the three returned values are assigned directly from the returned list into separate variables. This is a very nice feature of Python, allowing functions to effectively return multiple values.

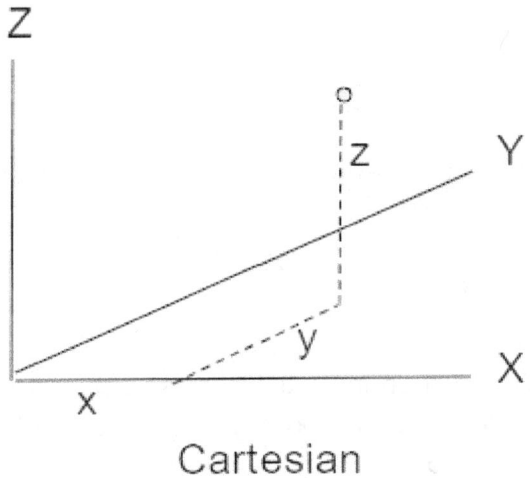

Cartesian

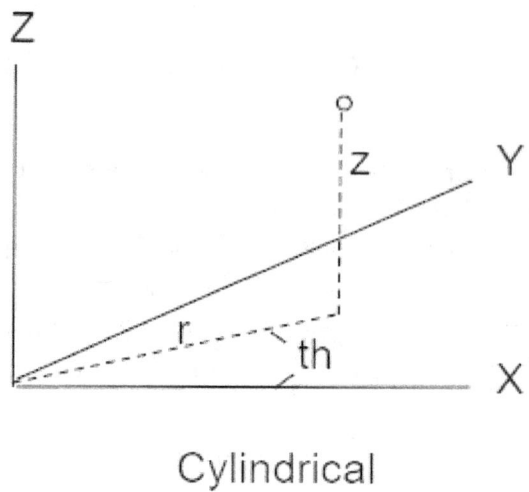

Cylindrical

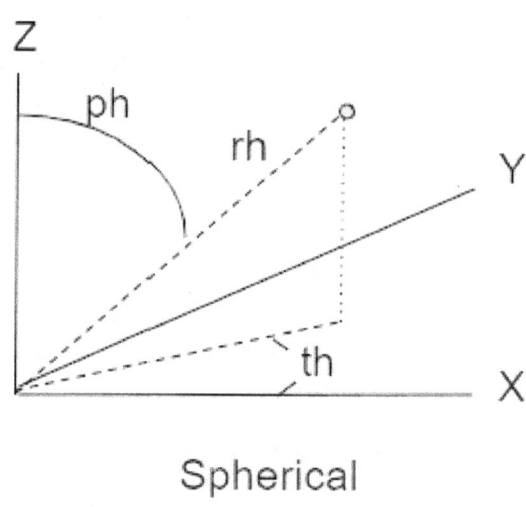

Spherical

For example, convert cartesian coordinate 3,4,5 to the other coordinate systems. When the program starts you are prompted to choose the known coordinate system, in this case Cartesian. As shown, enter a 1 to select that system, then enter 3, 4, and 5 as prompted for x, y, and z.

```
>>> from coord_3d import *
1. car->
2. cyl->
3. sph->
? 1
x: 3
y: 4
z: 5
```

After entering the final z value, the other two coordinate system equivalent values are calculated and displayed. If you need to refer back to the entered values, simply scroll up.

```
z:   5.0

cyl
ra:  5.0
th:  53.13010235415598
z:   5.0

sph
rh:  7.071067811865476
th:  53.13010235415598
ph:  45.00000000000001
>>>
```

```
# coord_3d.py
from math import *

def car_to_cyl(x,y,z):
  ra=(x*x+y*y)**.5
  th=degrees(atan2(y,x))
  return[ra,th,z]

def cyl_to_car(ra,th,z):
  th=radians(th)
  x=ra*cos(th)
  y=ra*sin(th)
  return [x,y,z]

def car_to_sph(x,y,z):
  rh=(x*x+y*y+z*z)**.5
  th=degrees(atan2(y,x))
  ph=degrees(acos(z/rh))
  return [rh,th,ph]

def sph_to_car(rh,th,ph):
  th=radians(th)
  ph=radians(ph)
  x=rh*sin(ph)*cos(th)
  y=rh*sin(ph)*sin(th)
  z=rh*cos(ph)
  return [x,y,z]

def cyl_to_sph(ra,th,z):
  rh=(ra*ra+z*z)**.5
  ph=degrees(atan2(ra,z))
  return [rh,th,ph]
```

```python
def sph_to_cyl(rh,th,ph):
    ph=radians(ph)
    ra=rh*sin(ph)
    z=rh*cos(ph)
    return [ra,th,z]

print("1. car->")
print("2. cyl->")
print("3. sph->")
n=int(input("? "))
if n==1:
    x=float(input("x: "))
    y=float(input("y: "))
    z=float(input("z: "))
    ra,th,z=car_to_cyl(x,y,z)
    rh,th,ph=car_to_sph(x,y,z)
```

```
    if n==2:
      ra=float(input("ra: "))
      th=float(input("th: "))
      z=float(input("z: "))
      x,y,z=cyl_to_car(ra,th,z)
      rh,th,ph=cyl_to_sph(ra,th,z)
    if n==3:
      rh=float(input("rh: "))
      th=float(input("th: "))
      ph=float(input("ph: "))
      x,y,z=sph_to_car(rh,th,ph)
      ra,th,z=sph_to_cyl(rh,th,ph)
print("\ncar")
print("x: ",x)
print("y: ",y)
print("z: ",z)
print("\ncyl")
print("ra: ",ra)
print("th: ",th)
print("z: ",z)
print("\nsph")
print("rh: ",rh)
print("th: ",th)
print("ph: ",ph)
```

rotate_3d.py

This program inputs a 3-dimensional point in space and rotates it around each of the three axes by some angle in degrees.

There are three functions in this program, one for rotating a space point around each axis. For demonstrating these functions, the input point is rotated around each, and the new location in each case is output.

These functions are at the core of many 3D graphics and other programs. I've used these functions to rotate antennas on the Earth to aim at geosynchronous satellites, and to rotate heliostats to reflect sunlight on solar energy targets.

For example, let's rotate the point (3,4,5) in space around each axis by 45 degrees:

```
>>> from rotate_3d import *
x: 3
y: 4
z: 5
rot deg: 45
```

The results fill the screen completely, so be sure to scroll if you need to see the input values.

```
deg                PYTHON
3.0
-0.707106781186547
6.363961030678928
roty:
5.65685424949238
4.0
1.414213562373095
rotz:
-0.707106781186547
4.949747468305833
5.0
>>>
```

```python
# rotate_3d.py
from math import *

def rotx(x,y,z,a):
  yn=y*cos(a)-z*sin(a)
  zn=y*sin(a)+z*cos(a)
  return [x,yn,zn]

def roty(x,y,z,a):
  xn=z*sin(a)+x*cos(a)
  zn=z*cos(a)-x*sin(a)
  return [xn,y,zn]

def rotz(x,y,z,a):
  xn=x*cos(a)-y*sin(a)
  yn=x*sin(a)+y*cos(a)
  return [xn,yn,z]
```

```python
x=float(input("x: "))
y=float(input("y: "))
z=float(input("z: "))
a=float(input("rot deg: "))
x2,y2,z2=rotx(x,y,z,radians(a))
print("rotx:")
print(x2)
print(y2)
print(z2)
x2,y2,z2=roty(x,y,z,radians(a))
print("roty:")
print(x2)
print(y2)
print(z2)
x2,y2,z2=rotz(x,y,z,radians(a))
print("rotz:")
print(x2)
print(y2)
print(z2)
```

triangles_3d.py

This program calculates the sides, angles, and the area of a triangle given three space coordinates.

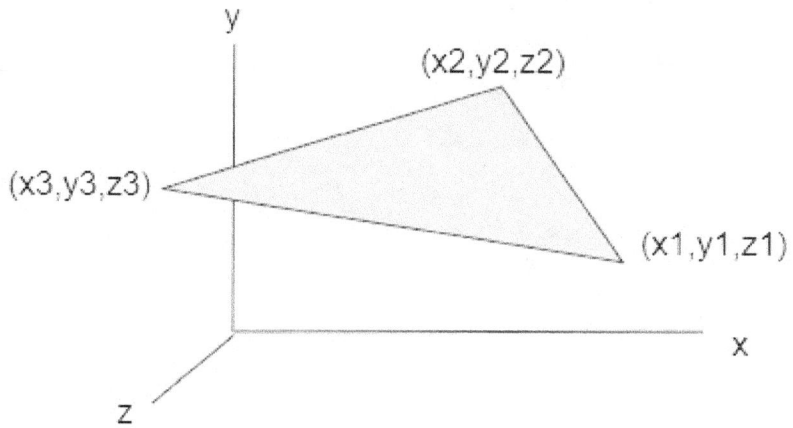

For example, given points (3,0,5), (4,2,2), and (0,1,3), find the lengths of the sides, the angles opposite each of the sides, and the area of the triangle.

Enter the value for all three coordinates, as prompted by the program:

```
>>> from triangles_3d import *
x1: 3
y1: 0
z1: 5
x2: 4
y2: 2
z2: 2
x3: 0
y3: 1
z3: 3
```

After entering the last value, the sides are displayed followed by the angles.

```
z2: 2
x3: 0
y3: 1
z3: 3
s(1-2):   3.741657386773941
s(1-3):   3.741657386773941
s(2-3):   4.242640687119285
a(1):   69.07516757236166
a(2):   55.46241621381917
a(3):   55.46241621381917
area:   5.766281297335398
>>>
```

The label s(1-2) indicates the side between points 1 and 2. The angle a(1) indicates the angle at the first coordinate entered.

```
# triangles_3d.py
from math import *

x1=float(input("x1: "))
y1=float(input("y1: "))
z1=float(input("z1: "))
x2=float(input("x2: "))
y2=float(input("y2: "))
z2=float(input("z2: "))
x3=float(input("x3: "))
y3=float(input("y3: "))
z3=float(input("z3: "))
```

```
a=((y2-y1)**2+(x2-x1)**2+(z2-z1)**2)**.5
b=((y3-y1)**2+(x3-x1)**2+(z3-z1)**2)**.5
c=((y3-y2)**2+(x3-x2)**2+(z3-z2)**2)**.5
B=degrees(acos((a*a+c*c-b*b)/a/c/2))
C=degrees(acos((b*b+c*c-a*a)/b/c/2))
A=180-B-C
area=a*b*sin(radians(C))/2
print("s(1-2): ",a)
print("s(1-3): ",b)
print("s(2-3): ",c)
print("a(1): ",A)
print("a(2): ",B)
print("a(3): ",C)
print("area: ",area)
```

volume_4p.py

Four cartesian points in space define a volume, in the shape of a stretched tetrahedron that has four triangular faces. This program calculates the volume of space inside this figure.

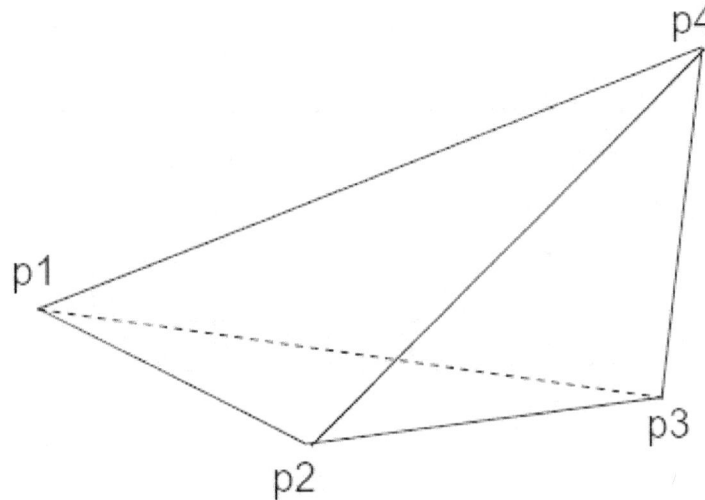

To keep the program simple the four space coordinates are set in the program listing, so you'll need to edit the program to set your own points. For the example demonstrated here, the points are set to [3,-2,5], [4,4,0], [6,3,7], and [6,5,0]. The calculated volume defined by these points is 9.5 cubic units.

This program uses a matrix calculation to find the volume. Here's the formula, and I encourage searching on the Internet to gain a better understanding how this matrix math works, and how in general working with matrices can simplify a lot of interesting calculations.

$$Volume = \frac{1}{6} \times \begin{vmatrix} 1 & x1 & y1 & z1 \\ 1 & x2 & y2 & z2 \\ 1 & x3 & y3 & z3 \\ 1 & x4 & y4 & z4 \end{vmatrix}$$

```
>>> from volume_4p import *
[3, -2, 5]
[4, 4, 0]
[6, 3, 7]
[6, 5, 0]
Vol: 9.5
>>>
```

```python
# volume_4p.py
from math import *

def vol(p1,p2,p3,p4):
  x0,y0,z0=p1
  x1,y1,z1=p2
  x2,y2,z2=p3
  x3,y3,z3=p4
  a=y1*z2+y2*z3+y3*z1
  b=y1*z3+y2*z1+y3*z2
  t0=x0*(a-b)
  a=x1*z2+x2*z3+x3*z1
  b=x1*z3+x2*z1+x3*z2
  t1=y0*(a-b)
  a=x1*y2+x2*y3+x3*y1
  b=x1*y3+x2*y1+x3*y2
  t2=z0*(a-b)
  a=x1*y2*z3+x2*y3*z1+x3*y1*z2
  b=x1*y3*z2+x2*y1*z3+x3*y2*z1
  t3=a-b
  return abs(t0-t1+t2-t3)/6
```

```
p1=[3,-2,5]
p2=[4,4,0]
p3=[6,3,7]
p4=[6,5,0]
print(p1)
print(p2)
print(p3)
print(p4)
print("Vol: ",vol(p1,p2,p3,p4))
```

9.

Space Sciences

How many "habitable zone" planets are predicted to be out there somewhere, each possibly capable of supporting organic life? How fast do you need to spin a space station to generate an artificial gravity effect? What did the phase of the moon look like on the day you were born?

These and many other interesting and challenging questions are covered by the programs in this chapter.

antenna_aim.py

Satellites orbit the Earth based on their distance from the Earth. The International Space Station is about 410 km up, and it takes about an hour and a half to complete each orbit, whereas the Moon is about 385,000 km away, and it takes roughly 27 days to complete one orbit.

Geosynchronous satellites orbit between these two extremes, at an altitude of about 35,786 km, where each orbit takes exactly one day. They are located above the equator, orbiting in the same direction that the Earth spins, with the result that they appear to stay in one spot above the Earth all the time.

This program asks for the location on the Earth of an antenna that is to be aimed at a geosynchronous satellite located at some specific longitude above the equator, and calculates how to aim it. Azimuth is the angle away from north along the horizon, where east is 90 degrees, south is 180 degrees, and so on. Elevation angle is up from the horizon, where 90 degrees would be directly overhead.

The sign of longitudes should match Google Maps locations. So west longitudes, such as in all of North America, are negative numbers, and satellites with a west longitude location are also to be entered as negative numbers.

For example, an antenna located in Roswell, NM is at 33.376 degrees north, and 104.508 degrees west. The goal is to aim it at the GOES-15 weather satellite located at 127.8 degrees west longitude. Enter the values as shown to determine that the antenna should be aimed south-west at 218.0 degrees azimuth, and at an elevation of 43.8 degrees up from the horizon.

```
>>> from antenna_aim import *
Ant lat: 33.376
Ant lon: -104.508
Sat lon: -127.8
Ant az:  218.0447965713992
Ant el:  43.83114435998777
>>>
```

```python
#antenna_aim.py
from math import *

la=radians(float(input("Ant lat: ")))
lo=radians(float(input("Ant lon: ")))
sl=radians(float(input("Sat lon: ")))
L=sl-lo
D=acos(cos(la)*cos(L))
az=degrees(acos(-tan(la)/tan(D)))
az=az if L>0 else 360-az
cd=cos(D)
el=degrees(atan((cd-1/6.62)/(1-cd*cd)**.5))
print("Ant az: ",az)
print("Ant el: ",el)
```

For a more detailed explanation of the math involved in this calculation, see the PDF document at https://tinyurl.com/y3d5lvng.

For a list of current geosynchronous satellites, go to https:/tinyurl.com/y2ahfmwe.

moon.py

Calculating the Moon and its current phase with high accuracy is extremely complicated. This program provides a very simplified approximation that is plenty accurate enough for most normal purposes. Any date in the years 1582 to 4000 can be input, and the percent lit from the Sun is output, plus an indication of "waxing" or "waning" to let you know which half of the month the Moon is in.

For example, describe the Moon's appearance from the Earth on the day men first landed on it, July 20, 1969.

```
>>> from moon import *
Month (1-12): 7
Day (1-31): 20
Year (1582-4000): 1969

Percent lit:   40
Waxing

>>>
```

The moon was a little less than half lit up, and each day more of the Moon was being lit (waxing). For a visual on what the Moon looked like on this date, see the related program moon_img.py.

```python
# moon.py
from math import *

def moon(m,d,y):
  j=jd(m,d,y)
  n=(j+5.367)/29.53058
  x=n-int(n)
  p=int(abs(2*(x)-1)*100)
  w=int(2*x)
  return [p,w]

def jd(m,d,y):
  if m<3:
    y-=1
    m+=12
  a=int(y/100)
  b=2-a+int(a/4)
  e=int(365.25*(y+4716))
  f=int(30.6001*(m+1))
  return b+d+e+f-1524.5

m=int(input("Month (1-12): "))
d=int(input("Day (1-31): "))
y=int(input("Year (1582-4000): "))
phase,wax=moon(m,d,y)
print("\nPercent lit: ",phase)
w="x" if wax else "n"
print("Wa{0}ing\n".format(w))
```

moon_img.py

This program uses the kandinsky module to draw the Moon's appearance on any date from the year 1582 to 4000. The moon.py program displays the same result in text format, whereas this program sketches the appearance of the Moon in the night sky. We'll use the same date in history, July 20, 1969, the day men first landed on the Moon, in both programs.

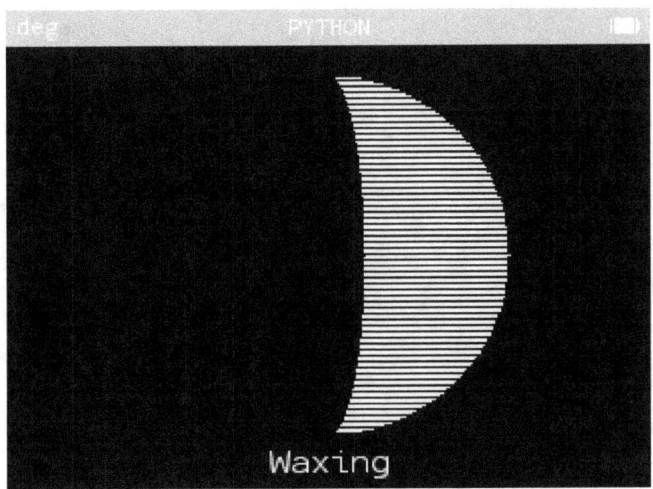

The kandinsky module doesn't provide a line drawing function, so this program draws long, thin horizontal rectangles that effectively create straight, horizontal lines. To emulate the bright, yet gray appearance of the Moon, only every other horizontal line is drawn.

If you want the Moon to be yellow, or any other color for that matter, experiment with the color() parameter in the fill_rect() function calls. Similarly, you can change the appearance of the text at the bottom edge of the Moon by experimenting with the last few code lines in the program.

```
# moon_img.py
from math import *
from kandinsky import *

def moon(m,d,y):
  j=jd(m,d,y)
  n=(j+5.367)/29.53058
  x=n-int(n)
  p=int(abs(2*(x)-1)*100)
  w=int(2*x)
  return [p,w]

def jd(m,d,y):
  if m<3:
    y-=1
    m+=12
  a=int(y/100)
  b=2-a+int(a/4)
  e=int(365.25*(y+4716))
  f=int(30.6001*(m+1))
  return b+d+e+f-1524.5

m=int(input("Month (1-12): "))
d=int(input("Day (1-31): "))
y=int(input("Year (1582-4000): "))
pct,wax=moon(m,d,y)
fill_rect(0,0,320,222,color(0,0,0))
n=60
for yi in range(-n,n):
  y=yi/n
  x2=(1-y*y)**.5
  x1=-x2
  if wax:
    xa=x2-(x2-x1)*pct/100
    xb=x2
```

```
    else:
      xa=x1
      xb=x1+(x2-x1)*pct/100
    xp=int(90*xa+160)
    yp=int(90*y+105)
    xn=int(90*(xb-xa))
    yn=1
    fill_rect(xp,yp,xn,yn,color(255,255,255))

w="Waxing" if wax else "Waning"
c1=color(255,255,255)
c2=color(0,0,0)
draw_string(w,130,200,c1,c2)
```

pennies.py

This program is a little different, in that no attempt was made to minimize the number of bytes in the source code. It also calculates something totally amazing, so putting in a lot of explanatory comments and very clear, rather long variable names felt like the right thing to do. If you feel the results are too bizarre to believe, please by all means double and triple check my calculations, and let me know what you discover.

Space is a very big place. Very big. I've researched and found the latest numbers for several important factors about stars, galaxies, and so on, and put reference links to places on the Internet where you can research for yourself. By the time you read this, some of these parameters will likely have been updated, so feel free to adjust the program as required.

The exact dimensions of a U.S. penny let us calculate the size of a stack we can pile so many of them into. For example, a million pennies can be stacked in neat rows and columns into a mass very roughly the size of a desk or refrigerator. Keep that in mind as we proceed.

This program uses the estimated number of stars per galaxy, the number of galaxies in the known Universe, and the number of planets being found around stars, and so on, to make a guess as to how many "habitable zone" planets are out there somewhere. This rules out planets that are probably too hot or too cold for life as we know it, but it turns out there are likely many planets that are "just right". Some sources call these "Goldilocks planets".

Follow through the calculations to see how big a stack of pennies would be if each penny represented one habitable zone planet. The answer is staggering!

```
>>> from pennies_metric import
If every earth-like planet
were a U.S. penny, you could
stack them to cover the total
continental U.S. land area to
a height of 8.5 km!
(or 5.3 miles)
>>>
```

```python
# pennies.py

# http://bit.ly/2Poq48E
# Dimensions of U.S. penny
diameter=19.05 # mm
thickness=1.52 # mm

# cubic millimeters per stacked penny
rect_vol=diameter*diameter*thickness

# cubic meters for one stacked penny
penny_vol=rect_vol*1e-9

# http://bit.ly/2Pqf8ao
# One in 4 stars has a goldilocks planet
goldilocks_factor=0.25

# http://bit.ly/2VmUkoc
# Two trillion galaxies
galaxies=2e12

# http://bit.ly/2TitCdt
# 250 billion stars in our avg sized galaxy
milky_way_stars=250e9
```

```python
# Total stars in the known universe
stars=galaxies*milky_way_stars

# Total habitable goldilocks planets
habitable_planets=stars*goldilocks_factor

# Cubic meters of pennies if same
# number as habitable planets
m3_pennies=habitable_planets*penny_vol

# http://bit.ly/2HUkZRd
# Area of continental United States
us_square_kilometers=8_080_464.3

# http://bit.ly/32qvRjj
# Convert area to square meters
us_m2=us_square_kilometers*1000*1000

# Meters height of all those pennies
# if covering all continental U.S.
height_in_meters=m3_pennies/us_m2

# Convert to kilometers
height_in_km=height_in_meters/1000

# http://bit.ly/3c7NdFT
# Also convert to U.S. miles...
height_in_miles=height_in_km*0.621371

# Output results
print("\nNumber of habitable zone")
print("planets: ",habitable_planets)
print()
print("If every earth-like planet")
print("were a U.S. penny, you could")
print("stack them to cover the total")
print("continental U.S. land area to")
km=round(height_in_km,1)
print("a height of",km,"km!")
mi=round(height_in_miles,1)
print("(or",mi,"miles)")
```

radioisotope.py

The speed of radioactive decays in a sample is proportional to the number of radioactive atoms in the sample. The heart of the required calculations involves differential equations, which you can read about online if interested. Perhaps you've heard of carbon-14 dating of ancient organic materials? This is how they do the math for that! But this program works with any radioisotope with a known half-life. For example, rocks returned from the Moon containing radioactive isotopes have allowed an estimation of its age.

This program works with four parameters, the starting activity of a sample, its half-life, elapsed time, and the ending activity of the sample. You input any combination of three of these parameters and the fourth is calculated.

For example, an isotope of chromium with a half-life of 667.2 hours has a starting activity of 200 microcuries. What will its activity be exactly 24 hours later?

```
>>> from radioisotope import *
Enter 3 known values...
Starting activity: 200
Half life: 667.2
Elapsed time: 24
Final activity: |
```

Note that the half-life might be in units of seconds, hours, or even years. Be sure to enter the elapsed time in the same, matching units. In this case both values are in hours.

```
 deg              PYTHON
 Starting activity:
200.0

 Half life:
667.2000000000001

 Elapsed time:
24.0

 Final activity:
195.0749833652744
>>>
```

The final activity, measured the next day, will be 195 microcuries.

```python
# Radioisotope.py
from math import *

print("Enter 3 known values...")
s1="Starting activity: "
s2="Half life: "
s3="Elapsed time: "
s4="Final activity: "
sa=input(s1)
sa=float(sa) if sa else 0
ha=input(s2)
ha=float(ha) if ha else 0
et=input(s3)
et=float(et) if et else 0
```

```
fa=input(s4)
fa=float(fa) if fa else 0
if not sa:
   sa=fa/.5**(et/ha)
if not ha:
   ha=et*log(.5)/log(fa/sa)
if not et:
   et=ha*log(fa/sa)/log(.5)
if not fa:
   fa=sa*.5**(et/ha)
print("\n",s1)
print(sa)
print("\n",s2)
print(ha)
print("\n",s3)
print(et)
print("\n",s4)
print(fa)
```

relativity.py

At very high velocity, what is called relativistic velocity, space and time start to get really weird. We don't notice the effects normally, because even the fastest space crafts we have move at only a tiny fraction of the speed of light. If they could move at the speed of light, they would orbit the Earth seven times every second.

At the heart of several relativistic calculations is gamma, a value calculated from a velocity V as compared to the speed of light C. Here's the formula for gamma:

$$\gamma = \frac{1}{\sqrt{1 - \frac{V^2}{C^2}}}$$

This program lets you input a velocity as a fraction of the speed of light. The actual velocity and the value of gamma is then calculated, and the distortion of time, length and mass is described. For example, if a spaceship could travel at 95% of the speed of light, here's what we'd observe from Earth:

```
V/C:   0.95

V (km/s):   284802.835
C (km/s):   299792.458

Gamma:   3.20256

For 'on-board' time and
length as observed from
Earth, divide by gamma.
For mass, multiply by gamma.
>>>
```

```python
# Relativity
print("\nFraction of speed of light")
f=float(input("? "))
g=1/(1-f**2)**.5
c=299792.458
v=c*f
print("\n\nV/C: ",f)
print("\nV (km/s): ",round(v,3))
print("C (km/s): ",c)
print("\nGamma: ",round(g,5))
print("\nFor 'on-board' time and")
print("length as observed from")
print("Earth, divide by gamma.")
print("For mass, multiply by gamma.")
```

station_gravity.py

In the movie Interstellar, the main characters start their wheel-shaped station spinning in space in order to generate an artificial gravity of one G, or the same acceleration as we experience on Earth from gravity. They spin up to a certain rotational velocity in order for the centrifugal force to reach one G.

So how fast do they need to spin their station? The three factors are spin rate, radius of the rotation, and the G force created at the circumference. This program lets you input any two of these, and the third is calculated.

Search "artificial gravity" in Wikipedia for a much more in-depth explanation of how this all works. If g is the number of Gs, r is the radius of spin, and s is the number of seconds for one complete rotation, then here's the formula that ties them all together:

$$\frac{g \cdot s^2}{r} = \frac{4 \cdot \pi^2}{9.8}$$

For example, I timed the rotation of the station shown in Interstellar with a stopwatch. It was spinning approximately 12 seconds per complete revolution. The main character stated they were then at one G, so how far out from the center of the rotation were they?

```
>>> from station_gravity impor

Radius of rotation (meters)
Seconds per rotation
Gs = normal gravity is 1.0

Enter all except for unknown

Radius:
Seconds/rot: 12
Gs of accel: 1
```

Just press OK when prompted for the unknown, in this case the Radius. Enter the other two values as shown, and the program shows a radius of about 36 meters.

```
Gs = normal gravity is 1.0

Enter all except for unknown

Radius:
Seconds/rot: 12
Gs of accel: 1

Radius:   35.74611358901677
Seconds/rot:   12.0
Gs of accel:   1.0
>>>
```

```
# station_gravity.py
from math import *

print("\nRadius of rotation (meters)")
print("Seconds per rotation")
print("Gs = normal gravity is 1.0")
print("\nEnter all except for unknown")
a="\nRadius: "
b="Seconds/rot: "
c="Gs of accel: "
r=input(a)
r=float(r) if r else 0
s=input(b)
s=float(s) if s else 0
g=input(c)
g=float(g) if g else 0
```

```
  if not r:
    r=9.8*g*s**2/(4*pi**2)
  if not s:
    s=2*pi/(9.8*g/r)**.5
  if not g:
    g=4*pi*pi*r/9.8/s**2
  print(a,r)
  print(b,s)
  print(c,g)
```

sun_elev.py

This program provides a simple way for you to measure the Sun's elevation angle. Use a meter or yard stick and measure its shadow on a flat surface. Plug the numbers in and the elevation angle is calculated using the atan() function in the math module.

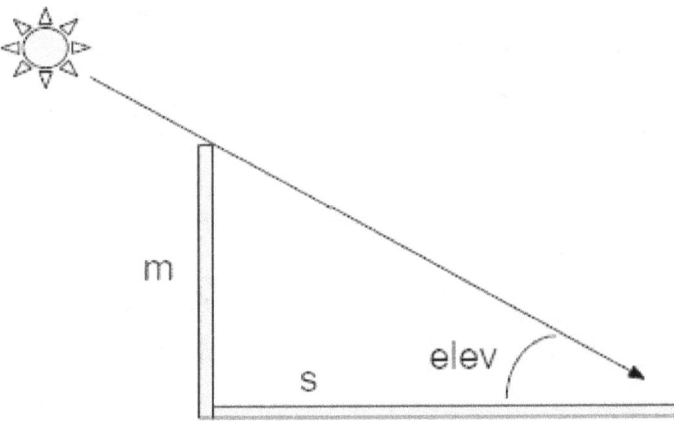

Be sure to use the same units for the object's height and the shadow length. For example, if a meter stick's shadow is 134 cm (1 meter is 100 cm) then the angle of elevation of the Sun is about 36.7 degrees.

```
>>> from sun_elev import *
Height of object: 100
Length of its shadow: 134
Sun elevation:  36.7
>>>
```

The atan() function, like the rest of the trigonometric functions in the math module, assumes all angles to be in radians. The degrees() function is used to convert the radians elevation angle to degrees.

```
# sun_elev
from math import *

h=float(input("Height of object: "))
s=float(input("Length of its shadow: "))
elev=degrees(atan(h/s))
print("Sun elevation: ",round(elev,1))
```

sun_loc.py

This program calculates the exact location on the Earth where the Sun is directly overhead at the zenith. The Sun is always shining somewhere, so this spot is constantly wandering all the way around the planet every 24 hours.

To demonstrate the sunloc() function, an exact date and time, including the timezone offset from Greenwich, is passed to the function in a list. The latitude and longitude of the Sun's zenith point on the Earth is returned in a list. The accuracy of the Sun's position using this algorithm is within about 0.01 degree of its true location.

For example, on the 4th of July, 2022 at 12:50:00 pm in Denver, CO (time zone offset is -6 hours from Greenwich) the Sun will be located at about 22.82 degrees north latitude and 101.37 degrees west longitude. A quick check on Google Maps shows this spot to be in the middle of Mexico, just north of San Luis Potosi.

```
>>> from sun_loc import *
When:    [2022, 7, 4, 12, 50, 0,
Sun lat:   22.82169970485554
Sun lon:  -101.3746963217855
>>>
```

```python
# sun_loc.py
from math import *

def sunloc(when):
    ye,mo,da,ho,mi,se,tz=when
    ta=pi*2
    ut=ho-tz+mi/60+se/3600
    t=367*ye-7*(ye+(mo+9)//12)//4
    dn=t+275*mo//9+da-730531.5+ut/24
    sl=dn*0.01720279239+4.894967873
    sa=dn*0.01720197034+6.240040768
    t=sl+0.03342305518*sin(sa)
    ec=t+0.0003490658504*sin(2*sa)
    ob=0.4090877234-0.000000006981317008*dn
    st=4.894961213+6.300388099*dn
    ra=atan2(cos(ob)*sin(ec),cos(ec))
    de=asin(sin(ob)*sin(ec))
    la=degrees(de)
    lo= degrees(ra-st)%360
    lo=lo-360 if lo>180 else lo
    return [la,lo]

when=[2022,7,4,12,50,0,-6]
la,lo=sunloc(when)
print("When: ",when)
print("Sun lat: ",la)
print("Sun lon: ",lo)
```

10.

Other Useful Programs

This chapter presents a few programs that were fun to create, but didn't neatly fit into any of the other chapters. One concrete example is a program that calculates the cubic yards of concrete. Another chilling example calculates wind chill index. There's even a secret program I won't tell you about here. Go discover it for yourself!

concrete.py

A very common problem with construction projects is to determine how many cubic yards of concrete to order. Typically, a driveway, sidewalk, or other area is measured in feet length and width, and inches in depth. This program takes these three values, does the proper conversions to common units, and multiplies them to get cubic yards.

A great challenge to test your Python programming skills is to change this program to use all metric units. I kept the units in feet, inches, and cubic yards to match the standard units used in the United States.

For example, the suggested thickness of a passenger car driveway is 4 inches. How many cubic yards of concrete will be required for a 12 foot wide driveway that is 15 feet long?

```
>>> from concrete import *
Concrete volume
Length (ft): 15
Width (ft): 12
Depth (in): 4
Cubic yards: 2.22
>>>
```

```python
# concrete.py
print("Concrete volume")
h=float(input("Length (ft): "))
w=float(input("Width (ft): "))
d=float(input("Depth (in): "))
yd=round(h*w*d/324,2)
print("Cubic yards:",yd)
```

laser_distance.py

If you have a little laser distance measuring device (they're a lot of fun) you can use it along with this program to measure distances along hard to reach lines.

For example, let's say you want to measure the height of a wall, from floor to ceiling, but you don't want to get on a ladder. You can measure the distance from your eye level, where you hold the laser device, to the floor, then to the wall in front of you at eye level, and then to the top edge of the wall. These are marked as points a, b, and c on this diagram:

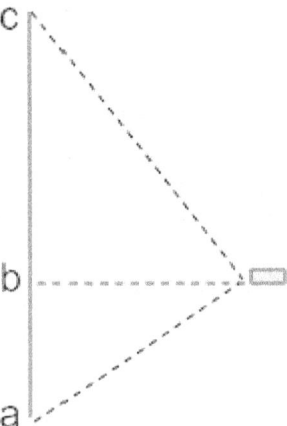

If the distance to a is 9 feet 3 inches, to b is 7 feet 9 inches, and to c is 12 feet 10 inches, then the program calculates the height of the wall from a to c as 14 feet 0 inches.

```
Enter 'ft in' to 3 pts in
a row, where one point is
perpendicular...

Distance a ... ft in: 9 3
Distance b ... ft in: 7 9
Distance c ... ft in: 12 6

Distance between the two
non-perpendicular points:
ft in:   14 10
>>>
```

Enter the three distances sequentially, in the order they appear along the line you are measuring. Even if the first or last measurement is the one that's perpendicular to the line, the distance between the non-perpendicular points will always be calculated correctly.

For example, let's say you have a giant painting on a high wall and you want to measure its height, something like measuring b to c in this diagram:

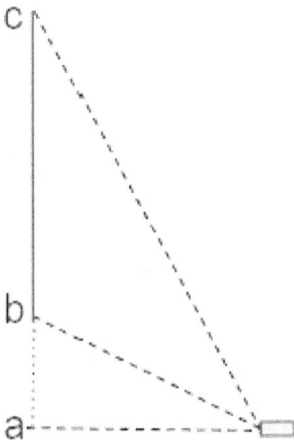

In this case enter the distance to a, b, and c in that order (or in c, b, a order - just keep them sequential along the line.) In this case the distance b to c will be calculated. Here's a sample run showing a calculated height from b to c of 10 feet 8 inches.

```
Enter 'ft in' to 3 pts in
a row, where one point is
perpendicular...

Distance a ... ft in: 8 1
Distance b ... ft in: 9 2
Distance c ... ft in: 17 0

Distance between the two
non-perpendicular points:
ft in:  10 8
>>>
```

```python
# laser_distance.py
print("Enter 'ft in' to 3 pts in")
print("a row, where one point is")
print("perpendicular...\n")

a=input("Distance a ... ft in: ")
a=(a.strip()+' 0').split()
a=float(a[0])+float(a[1])/12

b=input("Distance b ... ft in: ")
b=(b.strip()+' 0').split()
b=float(b[0])+float(b[1])/12
```

```python
c=input("Distance c ... ft in: ")
c=(c.strip()+' 0').split()
c=float(c[0])+float(c[1])/12

ft=0

if a>b and b<c:
   d=(a*a-b*b)**0.5
   e=(c*c-b*b)**0.5
   ft=d+e

if a<b and b<c:
   d=(b*b-a*a)**0.5
   e=(c*c-a*a)**0.5
   ft=e-d

if a>b and b>c:
   d=(b*b-c*c)**0.5
   e=(a*a-c*c)**0.5
   ft=e-d

feet=int(ft)
inch=round((ft-feet)*12)
print("\nDistance between the two")
print("non-perpendicular points:")
print('ft in: ',feet,inch)
```

secret.py

This program lets you encrypt and decrypt secret messages. The action is a little cumbersome, but for short messages, such as a password used elsewhere that you want to keep safe, this program does provide a fairly high level of security.

For example, let's encrypt the spy-talk phrase "The dew is on the roses" using a key of "abc123". First, select 1 to do an encryption, enter the phrase, then enter the key.

```
>>> from secret import *
1. Encrypt
2. Decrypt
? 1
Msg? The dew is on the roses.
Key? abc123
```

The encrypted data is displayed as blocks of four hexadecimal characters. That's the data you will write down and save away, or send to your spy buddy somewhere.

```
0B4A 90E5 AAB7 42F1
3B50 D04F 8D75 F353
E626 2FD5 FE0A A5C7

>>>
```

To decrypt the message, choose 2 to start a decryption. At each "Sec?" prompt enter one secret block of encrypted hexadecimal characters. Lower case is okay, and that actually makes it easier to type them in.

```
>>> from secret import *
1. Encrypt
2. Decrypt
? 2
Sec? 0b4a
Sec? 90e5
Sec? aab7
Sec? 42f1
Sec? 3b50
Sec? d04f
Sec?
```

Continue until all the code blocks are entered. Note that in some cases the last block might have fewer than four characters, but that's okay, just enter what was displayed after the encryption.

```
Sec? 42f1
Sec? 3b50
Sec? d04f
Sec? 8d75
Sec? f353
Sec? e626
Sec? 2fd5
Sec? fe0a
Sec? a5c7
Sec?

Key? abc123
```

Once the last block is entered, press [OK] one last time to get to the prompt for the Key. Enter the secret key (you and your spy buddy will keep this key secret), and the original message will pop up after a bit of processing.

```
                The dew is on the roses.
                >>>
```

```
# secret.py
m1=17
n1=23
m2=145
n2=87
a=[]

def rseed(s):
  for c in s:
    a.append(ord(c))
  for i in range(97):
    rbyte()

def rbyte():
  la=len(a)
  for i in range(la):
    j=(i+1)%la
    a[i]+=a[j]
    a[i]+=i*m1+n1
    a[i]+=j*m2+n2
    a[i]%=256
  return a[0]
```

```python
def hexchr(c):
    return ("0"+hex(c)[2:])[-2:].upper()

def chrhex(h):
    return eval("0x"+h)

def cls():
    print('\n'*20)

print("1. Encrypt")
print("2. Decrypt")
n=int(input("? "))
s=""
x=0
if n==1:
    msg=input("Msg? ")
    key=input("Key? ")
    rseed(key)
    for c in msg:
        b=ord(c)^rbyte()
        s+=hexchr(b)
        x+=1
        if not x%2:
            s+=' '
        if not x%8:
            s+='\n'
```

```
if n==2:
  sec=""
  x=1
  while x:
    x=input("Sec? ")
    sec+=x
  sec=sec.replace(' ','').upper()
  key=input("\nKey? ")
  rseed(key)
  i=0
  while i < len(sec):
    b=chrhex(sec[i:i+2])
    s+=chr(b^rbyte())
    i+=2
cls()
print(s)
```

wind_chill.py

When the wind blows, the air feels colder due to faster draining of heat from your body. There's a standard calculation for this wind chill factor, and this program handles it for you.

Enter the actual air temperature in degrees F, and the wind speed in miles per hour. The wind chill index is output. For example, at 30 mph, a real air temperature of 25F feels the same as 8F.

```
>>> from wind_chill import *
Temp (F): 25
Wind (mph): 30
Wind Chill Index: 8
>>>
```

```
# wind_chill.py
f=float(input("Temp (F): "))
w=float(input("Wind (mph): "))
v=w**.16
wc=35.74+.6215*f-35.75*v+.4275*f*v
print("Wind Chill Index:",round(wc))
```

About the author
John Clark Craig

John Clark Craig has authored many books on programming topics, mostly covering versions of BASIC and Visual Basic languages as they evolved over time.

Today his focus is on Python, the world's most popular and easy-to-learn language, suitable for introducing young people to programming for the first time, yet powerful enough for the most challenging engineering, web design, gaming, robotic and machine learning ... actually ALL of today's hot programming areas.

In addition to writing books, John's software projects have controlled and monitored huge solar energy projects, helped wind engineers design better towers for wind turbines, monitored natural gas and oil projects in Alaska, helped train athletes for the U.S.

Olympics teams, aided in the design of artificial knee replacement parts, provided a Python library for easier 3D design using OpenSCAD, and even provided tools for scientifically based research into the UFO phenomenon.

John lives in Colorado, today helping his wife with software tools that help her to help homeowners save lots of money by installing solar panels on rooftops. (See Solar-Proud.com)

Check out all his titles to show you just how passionate John is about the Python programming language and how it can be used in so many diverse ways to help others make the world a better place, one programming line at a time.

Other books by John Clark Craig

For a complete list of all the books
by John Clark Craig -
visit his website at

JohnClarkCraig.com

OpenSCAD Cookbook
OpenSCAD Recipes for learning 3D modeling -
ISBN: 1790273919

Python for 3D Printing
Using Python to enhance the power of OpenSCAD for 3D modeling -
ISBN: 1696881943

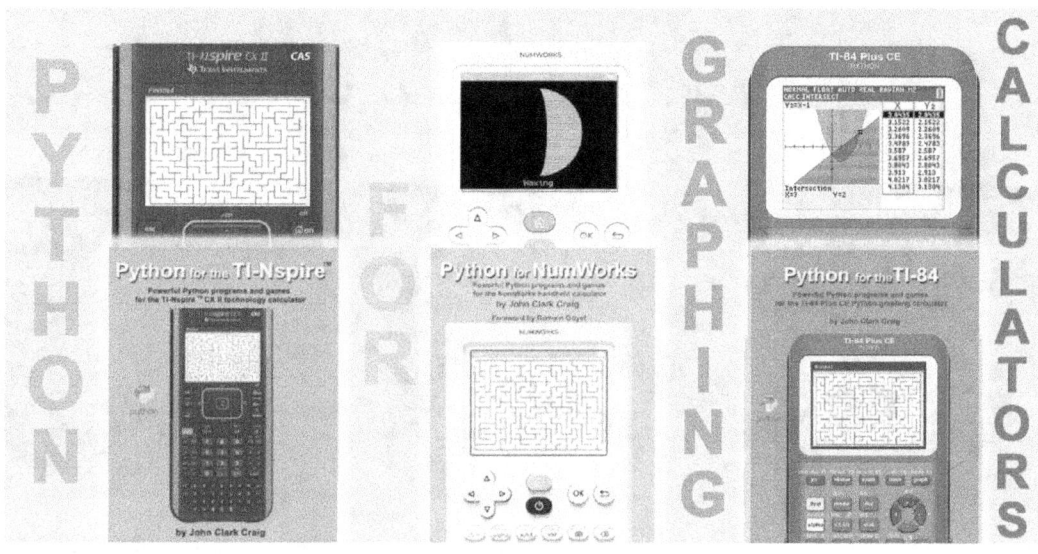

Python for NumWorks
Powerful Python programs and games for the NumWorks handheld calculator
ISBN: 979-8558337716

Python for the TI-Nspire™
Powerful Python programs and games for the TI-Nspire CX II technology calculator
ISBN: 979-8463835772

Python for the TI-84
Powerful Python programs and games for the TI-84 Plus CE Graphing Calculator
ISBN: 979-8476394686

Visual Basic (VB-2012) Programming By Example Series by John Clark Craig

VB-2012 - Random Numbers
introducing one of the best psuedorandom number generators
ASIN: B0075RJ42G

VB.NET - Sun Position
High accuracy solar position algorithms -
a resource for programmers and solar energy engineers
ASIN: B005AJ93F4

VB-2012 - Strings
programming examples of enhanced string processing
ASIN: B004G095MO

John's books from other publishers

Visual Basic 2005 Cookbook
John Clark Craig & Tim Patrick
O'Reilly

Microsoft Visual Basic: Developer's Workshop
John Clark Craig & Jeff Webb
Microsoft Press

For a complete list of all the books
by John Clark Craig -
visit his website at

JohnClarkCraig.com

To Contact John

for code downloads
to guest speak
or to consult:

email him at
john@craigware.com

www.ingramcontent.com/pod-product-compliance
Lightning Source LLC
Chambersburg PA
CBHW081425220526
45466CB00008B/2275